WORLD WAR 2
FOR YOUNG READERS

THE GREATEST BATTLES AND MOST HEROIC
EVENTS OF THE SECOND WORLD WAR

MARK BURTON

ISBN: 979-8-89095-012-3

TABLE OF CONTENTS

ATTENTION:

DO YOU WANT MY FUTURE BOOKS AT HEAVY DISCOUNTS AND EVEN FOR FREE?

HEAD OVER TO WWW.SECRETREADS.COM AND JOIN MY SECRET BOOK CLUB!

INTRODUCTION

Why did the world plunge into the biggest, bloodiest, most expensive war in its history? What led millions of men and women to sacrifice their lives and risk the total destruction of their nations? How could the world go so crazy?

The death toll from WWII is shocking.

The Soviet Union, a country that at the time contained Russia along with some smaller, now independent, nations like Lithuania and Ukraine, suffered nearly 24 million military and civilian deaths. Germany lost up to eight million dead. Italy, France, and the United Kingdom all lost over 450,000 people each. Nearly every country in Europe sacrificed thousands of lives in the conflict.

In Asia, China endured some 20 million military and civilian deaths. Japan lost over three million people. India too suffered more than three million deaths, according to some estimates.

The United States, fighting heavily in both Europe and Asia, sacrificed nearly 420,000 lives, mostly soldiers and sailors. Few civilians perished. Americans were lucky in this regard. The United States, by the end of the conflict in 1945, had not experienced the destruction of combat within its borders, except for a Japanese attack on a few remote islands in Alaska.

How did all this killing start?

The fighting in the Pacific Theater of WWII started in July 1937 when Imperial Japan pushed into China, unleashing a savage war that still influences relations between the two countries today. The desire of Imperial Japan to become the most powerful nation in the Pacific caused the country to later strike at the colonies of the United Kingdom, United States, France, and Holland in an effort to control the majority of the Pacific Ocean.

Headed by Hideki Tojo, the Japanese government and military were very devoted to their emperor, a man named Hirohito who was considered divine. The Imperial Japanese believed in the sacred power of their home island and considered themselves superior to other Asian peoples and equal to Westerners such as the Americans, British, Germans, and French. In fact, since the late 19th century, the Imperial Japanese had modeled the modernization and industrialization of their country on the United States and Germany.

By 1941, the leadership of Imperial Japan believed it needed to drive the United States completely out of the Pacific Ocean, restricting the Americans to the coasts of California, Oregon, and Washington. American soldiers stationed in the Philippines, Guam, and other islands claimed by the United States as territories threatened Japan's dreams of expansion and dominance over its neighbors.

The timing was right for Japan's military leaders. European countries like France, Holland, and the United Kingdom - all with colonies in the Pacific - were distracted by Nazi Germany. These countries were fighting for their homelands and could spare little effort defending territories on the other side of the globe. Only the United States seemed a threat to Imperial Japan.

Japanese military leaders gambled on an all-out surprise attack on the main battle fleet of the United States docked at

Pearl Harbor, Hawaii, on December 7, 1941. From that date until Imperial Japan's surrender was announced on August 15, 1945, Americans fought in a brutal war waged across the Pacific Ocean.

Events in the Pacific were linked to events in Europe, where the nations at war spread the conflict into Northern Africa and the Middle East. Imperial Japan and Nazi Germany were in an alliance known as the Axis, an alliance these two powers dominated. They were joined by Italy and several other countries such as Hungary, Romania, and Bulgaria along with a few small puppet regimes.

The fighting in the European Theater of WWII started in 1939 when Nazi Germany launched a surprise invasion of Poland. The Nazis, a political party led by Adolf Hitler, controlled the government and military. They wanted to expand Germany's borders and make the country the most powerful in Europe.

The Nazis were national socialists, meaning they supported socialism but only for the benefit of Germans. The government extended programs and aid to Germans but not to people considered by the Nazis to be racially or genetically inferior. Those people seen as inferior were attacked as a drain on the nation. The Nazis especially classified persons of Jewish ancestry as impure and in need of extermination.

In short, Nazi Germany was a fascist country. This meant that it was a dictatorship with a very centralized government that celebrated the nation as one based on its racial superiority.

But even before the Nazi German invasion of Poland in 1939, rumblings of war shook Europe as Axis countries asserted themselves. Italy, also a fascist regime under a man named

Benito Mussolini, had invaded Ethiopia along the Red Sea in Africa. This war raged from October 1935 until Italy's victory in February 1937.

A vicious civil war in Spain erupted from July 1936 until April 1939, suggesting a larger war across Europe might be brewing. There, the lawfully elected government fought a doomed struggle against fascist forces led by Francisco Franco. The armies of Franco received aid from Hitler and Mussolini. The Soviet Union sent supplies to the government. Several thousand volunteers from the United States enlisted in the failed effort to defeat Franco. The war resulted in an estimated 500,000 dead.

Overall, WWII killed nearly 4% of the world's population. The conflict turned into a massive global struggle between the totalitarian regimes of the Axis countries and the democratic regimes of the Allied nations. The latter was joined by the communists of the Soviet Union, who argued for a world of shared wealth for all managed through a centralized government. This communist government tightly controlled the economy.

The Allies maintained an uneasy alliance. The democratic Western nations were grounded by capitalism. They believed governments should take a mostly hands-off approach to the economy. This made for a natural distrust between the capitalist countries of the United States, United Kingdom, and France, on the one hand, and the communists within the Soviet Union, on the other hand. But the threat of the Axis regimes united the two groups as the Allies.

The high cost of lives created a new world order, one that still defines relationships between countries today. As the smoke of battle cleared, new organizations were formed, like the United Nations and World Bank, to ensure that another bloody conflict on the scale of WWII would not happen again. Also, because of WWII, the United States emerged as the so-called leader of the free world.

How WWII created the world we live in today calls for understanding how the war was fought, how it ended, and the role of the United States during this massive conflict.

A WORLD IN CHAOS

Adolf Hitler, a rising political leader in Germany, announced to an audience in March 1929: "If men wish to live, then they are forced to kill others," Hitler explained, "one is either the hammer or the anvil. We confess that it is our purpose to prepare the German people again for the role of the hammer."

For Americans, the Nazis were still a fringe group and their leader Hitler seemed a crank. He was a small man with an odd mustache who had been a failed artist and then a corporal in WWI.

Hitler a few years later organized the Nazi Party and attempted a coup to overthrow the Weimar Republic, the name given to the democratic German government established after WWI. The coup failed. Hitler was imprisoned, and in 1925, he wrote his manifesto *Mein Kampf* in prison before being released.

As Hitler attempted to gain clout in Germany in March 1929, Americans were enjoying good times. The idea of a global war erupting - one even more destructive than WWI - seemed impossible.

The decade of the 1920s became known as the Jazz Age because of the style of music popular at the time. Many Americans experienced great prosperity coming out of WWI, which ended in 1918. The war that raged across Europe for four years had caused France, the United Kingdom, and Germany, once the richest countries in the world, to fall heavily into debt. Often, their debt ended up being held by the United States, which sold goods and gave loans to these countries.

Part of this prosperity within the United States came from the popular new technologies changing American culture during the 1920s. The phonograph brought recorded music into homes. The radio broadcasted the latest news, sports events, and bands. Movies, first silent and - by the end of the 1920s - with sound, introduced Hollywood glamor to people's lives. Electric fans kept people cooler. Electric vacuum cleaners kept houses cleaner.

Though often invented decades earlier, the mass production of these technologies in the 1910s and 1920s made them cheaper. Homes were electrified to allow customers to use these technologies. All this created a massive change within American culture as electric devices gave more access to entertainment and made household tasks easier.

Perhaps the most important invention changing American lives was the automobile. The gas-guzzling cars of the 1920s, especially the affordable Model T built by Henry Ford, allowed a freedom Americans had never known. A journey of 10 or 20 miles that might previously have taken all day now took less than an hour! A road trip to Southern California or Florida became possible for not just the wealthy but anyone with a car and some spare money to pay for gas.

The car was especially important for linking the countryside to the big cities. Many even decided to leave their farms and move to urban areas. One of the biggest changes in the United States after WWI was that more Americans lived in cities than in the countryside for the first time in the country's history, according to the census taken in 1920.

All this care-free prosperity rested on a false confidence in global peace. A victorious member of the Allies coming out of WWI, the United States worked to end any wars forever, even though it refused to ratify the Versailles Treaty, which controversially forced Germany to accept sole responsibility for starting the conflict that people at the time called the Great War.

During the 1920s, the United States tried to limit the ability of nations to build militaries. The American government especially focused on global navies since much of Europe, and increasingly Japan, competed for colonies around the world. The Washington Naval Conference in 1922 set limits on the navies of the United States, United Kingdom, France, Italy, and Japan. The major powers of the world also declared an open door for trading with China. This seemed to solve some of the most heated issues after WWI.

When France later contacted the United States in 1928 to sign a treaty outlawing war between the two allies, American officials quickly wrote back that such a treaty should outlaw war everywhere and be signed by everyone. The Kellogg-Briand Pact, named for US Secretary of State Frank Kellogg and French Foreign Minister Aristide Briand, was signed by 57 countries within a year.

The Pact would clearly fail over the next decade, but the treaty remains in effect. It continues to serve as a foundation for preventing aggressive actions by nations and provides a reminder that countries need to pursue peaceful means for resolving disputes.

But, despite all the hope for a better, more prosperous future, the good times and faith in peace would not last.

In October 1929, the stock market crashed. The prosperity felt by many Americans had led them to make foolish investments in real estate and stocks. They had bought many of the new, mass-produced technologies on credit, meaning they went into debt. When prices of property and stocks plunged, people panicked and went broke. The Great Depression had started.

The Great Depression plunged the United States, and the world, into an age of doubt and fear. Americans faced widespread job losses.

By 1932, roughly 25% of the workforce in the United States was unemployed. For people of color, the unemployment rate skyrocketed to 50%. Hoovervilles appeared in every American city. These villages were built from scraps gathered by families kicked out of their homes after failing to pay their mortgages or rent. The name Hoovervilles referred to President Herbert Hoover, who failed to recognize the seriousness of the economic crisis.

Equally shocking was the crisis emerging in the rural United States during the 1930s. A severe drought descended upon the central portion of the country, causing massive dust storms that suffocated people and animals. Dust fell even as far away as Washington, D.C. From Texas to Montana, crops died and people fled. Some loaded their cars and journeyed to California looking for jobs, an exodus that caused the state to set up roadblocks to keep them out.

Eager for change, Americans elected Franklin Delano Roosevelt, the governor of New York, as President in 1932. He won in a landslide on a platform promising help and reform.

President Roosevelt spearheaded a program called the New Deal. The federal government stabilized banks. It created programs to employ jobless Americans. People working for these programs built infrastructure like roads, airports, and parks. Some surveyed historic architecture and interviewed Americans to preserve the history of the United States. Roosevelt's New Deal was so popular that he easily won the next elections in 1936, 1940, and 1944 - the only President elected to more than two terms.

In Europe, the Great Depression pitched Germans toward the Nazis. Already the fascist leader, Benito Mussolini, had seized control of Italy in the 1920s, paving the way for other rightwing movements across Europe. Now the Germans too became a dictatorship led by Hitler.

Hitler seized power in the early 1930s promising to restore Germany as a strong nation. He promised to provide cheap cars, offering the Volkswagen - the People's Wagon - as a competitor to Ford's Model T. He used radio and film to appeal to the German people with stories and images of empowerment and greatness. He also appealed to racism and other hatreds, telling Germans that the hardships in the country could be linked to people of Jewish ancestry, gay people, communists, and other groups.

His Nazis used violence to intimidate targeted groups, gathering them into urban ghettos or concentration camps. On an infamous day in November 1938, Nazi thugs smashed Jewish-owned stores and homes, beating and sometimes murdering Jewish families found inside. The day is now known as Kristallnacht, translated as "Crystal Night" for all the broken glass left on the streets. Some 30,000 Jews were gathered and put into concentration camps. Millions more followed them in the coming years as the Nazi regime passed laws to destroy Jews and their culture.

Instead of being horrified, most Germans saw the attacks on Jews as an opportunity to loot. A journalist remarked in the days after Kristallnacht that "the mobs gloated over the smashed stores of Jews. They helped themselves to clothes, furs, and toys, and scattered the goods in the streets for friends to pick up." The police ignored the vandalism and violence. Officers "walked unconcernedly through the havoc-bent crowds as if everybody was out for an enjoyable afternoon stroll."

Along with violence against targeted groups, Hitler ignored restrictions placed on Germany in the treaty ending WWI. He enlarged the military. He pushed troops into a neutral demilitarized along the Rhine River in western Germany. He seized Austria without a fight in March 1938.

In the United Kingdom and France, the Great Depression divided the population. Some looked with admiration at Mussolini and Hitler, believing their ideas were the key to the future. The racist policies of Mussolini and Hitler, as they worked to construct nations built upon supposedly pure bloodlines of Italians and Germans, made sense to some French and Britons.

Other Britons and French eyed socialism and communism, admiring the Soviet Union with its claims of equality for all and government programs that eliminated poverty. Born out of the collapse of Russia during WWI, the Soviet Union seemed to be making great economic strides, especially as the formerly prosperous Western democracies struggled during the Great Depression. But the French and Britons who favored the Soviet model often ignored the deadly policies endured by those living under the totalitarian regime run by leader Joseph Stalin (*Joseph Vissarionovich Stalin*).

All this division of political opinion paralyzed the governments of the United Kingdom and France as they worked to avoid tipping too far to the left or the right. This meant that neither stood up to Hitler as he pushed his agenda of building Nazi Germany into the greatest power in the world.

At the Munich Conference in 1938, British Prime Minister Neville Chamberlain negotiated with Hitler rather than confront him. Chamberlain allowed Hitler to seize the Sudetenland, an area with a high population of ethnic Germans, from Czechoslovakia. In return, Hitler promised to stop seizing any more territory. But he lied.

Hitler soon after negotiated the Molotov-Ribbentrop Pact, a secret non-aggression deal with Joseph Stalin of the Soviet Union.

The Pact divided Poland between them, with the Soviets being allowed a portion of eastern Poland after Germany conquered the country. The Nazi regime now invaded their eastern neighbor, fully aware that France and the United Kingdom had guaranteed Poland's survival. Both declared war on Nazi Germany but took little action.

In early 1940, the Nazis turned against the countries of Western Europe. Germany conquered Denmark and Norway. They marched into Holland and Belgium. Then they pushed into France. On June 22, 1940, France surrendered.

The German tactic called 'blitzkrieg' quickly overwhelmed the militaries of these countries. Blitzkrieg used tanks and mechanized infantry with air support - all new technologies in modern warfare.

Only the United Kingdom remained standing against the Nazis.

All the while, President Roosevelt looked on with concern as the world descended into armed conflict. Americans were divided. Some wanted to fight; others wanted to send aid only. Many argued that the United States should stay neutral.

Roosevelt watched, waited, and prepared the country for what he believed was unavoidable - the United States at some point would have to fight the Axis nations.

Across the Atlantic, Roosevelt looked for every means to keep the United Kingdom in the fight against Nazi Germany because the Britons shielded the United States from a possible attack. I

n September 1940, the President gave the United Kingdom, now led by Winston Churchill, 50 US destroyers in return for US access to British naval bases in the Atlantic. In March 1941, Roosevelt signed the Lend-Lease Act, allowing the United States to give food, oil, and war materiel to nations considered vital to Americans' safety.

Across the Pacific, Roosevelt observed the brutal war of expansion fought by Imperial Japan in China. He hoped an oil embargo might slow the Japanese. Instead, the Japanese now searched for an opportunity to hit the Americans so they could then seize oil fields in the South Pacific.

Did You Know . . .

- Henry Ford instructed that the Model T only come in the color black. He chose that color because black paint dried fastest, meaning that he could produce more vehicles on the assembly line. Between 1908 and 1927, the Ford Motor Company produced 15 million Model T cars. The US population in 1920 was 106 million.
- The most celebrated sports icon of the 1920s and 1930s was baseball star Babe Ruth of the New York Yankees. He is widely seen as the first celebrity athlete in the United States, even pioneering the Hollywood cameo when he briefly appeared in the comedy *Speedy*, about the hectic pace of life in the modern American city and starring Harold Lloyd, in 1928.
- The first movie to contain sound recording was *The Jazz Singer* in 1927. The film featured popular singer Al Jolson, a Lithuanian immigrant of Jewish ancestry. The character played by Jolson leaves behind traditional ways to embrace the modernity symbolized by jazz.
- In May 1927, Charles Lindbergh became the first person to fly alone across the Atlantic Ocean, from Long Island, New York, to Paris, France. The flight took just over 33 hours. Lindbergh became an international hero, showing that aviation was speeding travel around the world. Air power would play a major role in WWII.
- Frank Kellogg won the Nobel Peace Prize in 1929 for his role in creating the Kellogg-Briand Pact. He was the fifth

American to win the Prize. The first American to do so was President Theodore Roosevelt in 1906 for his role in ending a war between Russia and Japan.

- Filmed in December 1939, the wildly popular comedy trio called the Three Stooges made the first Hollywood film making fun of Adolf Hitler and the Nazis. Entitled *You Nazty Spy*, the 18-minute movie appeared nine months before Charlie Chaplin's much more famous comedy *The Dictator*.

PEARL HARBOR

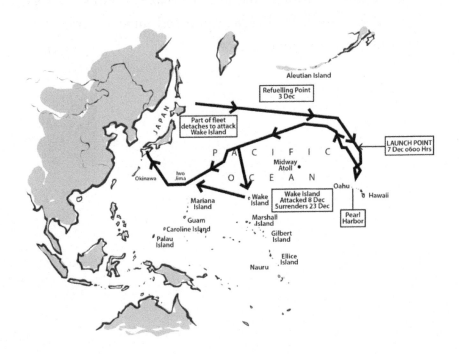

President Franklin Roosevelt approached the microphone to speak to the nation: "Yesterday, December 7, 1941 - a date which will live in infamy - the United States of America was suddenly and deliberately attacked by naval and air forces of the Empire of Japan." Radios relayed these stunning words to millions of Americans.

The President reassured the nation. Roosevelt knew hardship and struggle. He could only walk with the help of heavy braces after polio had paralyzed his legs in the early 1920s. The President promised, "No matter how long it may take us to overcome this premeditated invasion, the American people in their righteous might will win through to absolute victory.... With confidence in our armed forces - with the unbounding determination of our people - we will gain the inevitable triumph - so help us, God."

Roosevelt's anger and confidence disguised his worries. The Imperial Japanese Navy had either severely crippled or dropped to the bottom of Pearl Harbor much of the United States battleship fleet in the Pacific Ocean.

The daring strike, spearheaded by a fleet of Japanese aircraft carriers, was a gamble. Admiral Isoroku Yamamoto, the commander of the Japanese Navy, organized the surprise raid. He told an assistant as he worked on the plan that "we will have no hope of winning unless the United States fleet in Hawaiian waters can be destroyed."

Yamamoto knew the dangers of attacking the United States. He had joined a delegation of Japanese officers who visited the US Naval Academy in the 1920s. His tour led him to appreciate the size of the United States and its industrial strength.

As Imperial Japan looked to remove the United States as an obstacle to its ambitions in the Pacific, Yamamoto went to work designing the attack. The goal was to cripple the ability of the United States to counter an all-out offensive by Japan throughout the Pacific Ocean.

Military thinkers at the time believed the core of any nation's navy to be its battleships. Yamamoto therefore would sink the US battleship fleet. Time was key. Japan needed to expand into all the territory it wanted to control before the United States could rebuild the expensive, large vessels and whatever other ships it would need to launch a counterattack. Yamamoto hoped that the assault on Pearl Harbor would be such a shock that maybe Americans would opt to negotiate a compromise rather than try to fight.

If Americans did choose war, Yamamoto planned for the Japanese military to push as fast as possible southward toward the Dutch East Indies and Malaya. The rich oilfields in this area, in what today is Indonesia and Malaysia, would fuel the Japanese war machine - tanks, trucks, planes, and other equipment of modern warfare. Capturing these areas, along with Singapore and Southeast Asia, what is today Vietnam, Laos, and Cambodia, were the chief goals.

The Japanese would then dig-in, creating strong defensive positions to defeat any attacks by the United States. In a prolonged, bloody war, Yamamoto expected the Americans to lose the will to fight.

All of this centered on the ability of Yamamoto to do the incredible. He needed to sneak Japan's six aircraft carriers over 4,000 miles to Hawaii without being detected by patrolling US submarines or aircraft. The US military in Hawaii, sitting some 2,400 miles from California, had a false sense of security. Commanders at Pearl Harbor did not believe the Japanese Navy could reach them.

Once in position, the Imperial Japanese fleet launched two attack wings with a total of more than 353 aircraft. For 75 minutes on the morning of December 7, 1941, the planes, armed with torpedoes, bombs, and machine guns, pummeled the US fleet and support crews in Hawaii. As the Japanese planes headed back to their carriers for the return trip to Japan, the Americans counted their losses. Over 2,400 people, including 68 civilians, were dead. A total of 19 US Navy vessels were severely damaged, including four battleships sunk. Over 300 combat aircraft were damaged or destroyed, most of them while parked.

Yamamoto's plan had so far worked.

But even after an incredibly successful attack on Pearl Harbor, Yamamoto worried. He wrote in his diary after the strike: "I fear all we have done is to awaken a sleeping giant and fill him with a terrible resolve."

To prepare for that awakened giant, Japanese armies and navies were advancing. They attacked Malaya, the Philippines, Guam, Wake Island, Hong Kong, and numerous other points. Soon they pressed into the Dutch East Indies. By May 1942, the

Japanese even threatened the naval supply lines to Australia. They seemed unstoppable.

For the Americans, the shock of Pearl Harbor worsened with each passing day. On December 11, 1941, Hitler announced that Nazi Germany had declared war on the United States. Americans now faced a two-front war, one in the Pacific Theater against Japan and one in the European Theater against Germany, Italy, and other Axis nations there.

But with the Atlantic Ocean as a buffer and the Axis fleets of Europe bottled up by the British Navy, the United States could concentrate for the first year of the war on Japan.

News from the Philippines was especially troubling. The Japanese forces were rapidly closing on Manila, the capital, in the days after Pearl Harbor. Thousands of US soldiers were stationed nearby. With the US Pacific fleet crippled, a rescue of the Americans and Filipino allies was impossible.

For months, the American and Filipino armies resisted. They made a last stand on a fortified island called Corregidor under US General Douglas MacArthur. The troops, surrounded and under siege, suffered relentless bombardment.

President Franklin Roosevelt ordered MacArthur to leave his men behind. MacArthur was extremely reluctant to abandon his army. But Roosevelt wanted the general to relocate to Australia and prepare a plan for halting, then driving back, the Japanese military. Also, the President knew that the capture of the highly experienced MacArthur would worsen American morale and the nation's hope for the future.

MacArthur reluctantly escaped aboard a small but fast-moving patrol boat, slipping past the blockading Japanese fleet.

When he reached Australia, he went on the radio to broadcast to the Filipino people his promise that he would see to their eventual liberation: "I came through and I shall return."

MacArthur's army of American and Filipino soldiers was not so lucky. Roughly 15,000 Americans and 60,000 Filipinos surrendered on April 9, 1942. They were ordered to trek almost 65 miles to various prison camps on what became known as the Bataan Death March. Those too tired to make the long march or who became ill along the way were executed. Many were beaten. Over 500 Americans died. As many as 18,000 Filipinos perished according to some estimates.

Again, Yamamoto's grand strategy for the Pacific seemed to be working. But the age of the battleship had already passed. Yamamoto should have known better given the devastating effects of torpedo planes and dive bombers launched from aircraft carriers at Pearl Harbor. Fleets of battleships, cruisers, and other ships without air cover were sitting ducks.

As much as Yamamoto planned, he had overlooked the importance of destroying the American aircraft carriers in the Pacific Ocean. The three US carriers in the Pacific were out ferrying supplies to various naval outposts during the attack on Pearl Harbor.

Now those carriers, joined by more carriers brought from the Atlantic fleet, struck back. They participated in a daring attack on Tokyo, the capital of Japan.

The US military scrambled to boost American morale and show Imperial Japan that the Americans were not knocked out despite the defeats at Pearl Harbor and Corregidor. They turned to James Doolittle, a pioneering aviator.

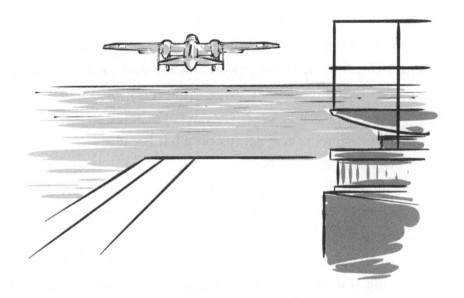

Doolittle's plan was a one-way bombing raid aimed at Tokyo. And every one of the 80 airmen who volunteered knew that their survival was doubtful.

Doolittle proposed stripping 16 land-based bombers known as B-25 Mitchells. The planes had to be light enough to carry extra fuel and a bomb payload while still being able to launch from an aircraft carrier.

The idea was crazy. The planes had to liftoff into high winds right as the carrier pitched upward from the waves to give the bombers a chance to avoid plunging from the carrier's runway straight into the Pacific Ocean.

The Doolittle Raid was scheduled for April 18, 1942. Two aircraft carriers would take the B-25s to within 2,400 miles of mainland Japan. The bombers, with a normal range of 1,300 miles, needed to carry twice the normal fuel load. Six hours after launch, the bombers arrived at Tokyo at noon. The bombers dropped their payload and then headed to China, where they ditched their planes. One bomber, very low on fuel, headed for the Soviet Union.

The Doolittle Raid had been successful. Miraculously, only three airmen had died. Eight were taken prisoner, but three of them were immediately executed.

The bombing caused little damage to Tokyo. The US military mainly wanted to show the Japanese that it too could carry out a surprise strike like the one the Japanese military had carried out at Pearl Harbor only four months earlier.

Little did the American commanders realize the fury within the Japanese military. The Doolittle Raid had largely been symbolic - a demonstration of US military know-how.

But the Japanese military now made plans to destroy the United States Navy once and for all. This decision would change the course of the war in the Pacific at an island called Midway.

Did You Know . . .

- Roughly half the deaths at Pearl Harbor came from the battleship *USS Arizona*, which sank when a bomb detonated one of its magazines full of ammunition. The *USS Arizona* was refueled with 1.5 million gallons of oil the day before the Japanese attack. Ever since it sank, the battleship has leaked around a quart of oil each day.

- The Japanese planned for five mini-submarines, each carrying two sailors armed with two torpedoes, to sail into Pearl Harbor as part of the attack. Only one made it into the harbor. The destroyer *USS Ward*, firing the first shots between the United States and Japan, quickly sank the submarine.

- One of the five mini-subs sent by Japan toward Pearl Harbor washed ashore in Hawaii the day after the attack. The submarine toured the United States to fundraise for the American war effort. This submarine is now on permanent display at the National Museum of the Pacific War in Fredericksburg, Texas.

- The United States repaired and raised all the battleships from the Pearl Harbor attack within six months. Only the *USS Oklahoma* and *USS Arizona* were unsalvageable. The Japanese had failed to attack the repair facilities and drydocks. Today, the *USS Arizona* is a memorial site.

- Kaname Harada, the last surviving Japanese combat pilot to attack Pearl Harbor, died on May 3, 2016. He suffered from lifelong nightmares of the war. To atone for the violence, after the war, Harada opened a kindergarten and became a vocal peace activist.

- In 1959, Hawaii became the 50th state to join the United States. Alaska gained statehood earlier that year. A popular television show about the state police in Hawaii, called *Hawaii 5-0*, aired from 1968–1980 and again from 2010–2020. The name referenced Hawaii as the 50th state, with the term "5-0" becoming slang for police everywhere in the United States.

MIDWAY

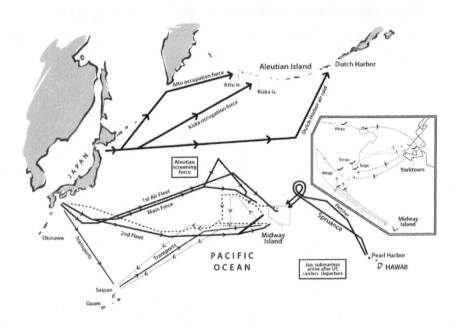

A tense journalist huddled aboard the *USS Yorktown,* one of the finest aircraft carriers in the American fleet, as Japanese bombers rained explosives on the ship's deck, later described the scene: "Every gun in the force was yammering away at the enemy planes as they plummeted, black as hate, out of the white clouds. The whole starboard side of the Yorktown seemed to burst into flame as her gunners poured out red-hot shells at the enemy bombers...."

The *USS Yorktown* had rushed full-throttle to Midway as part of a trap now closing on the Imperial Japanese Navy.

The man who designed the trap was Admiral Chester Nimitz. President Roosevelt promoted the experienced naval officer to the Commander-in-Chief of the US Pacific Fleet days after the attack on Pearl Harbor. Whereas General MacArthur would command the army forces in the Pacific, Nimitz would oversee the navy.

Luckily for Nimitz, codebreakers had figured out the encrypted messages used by the Imperial Japanese Navy. What they learned sprung Nimitz into action. The Japanese fleet was preparing an attack to capture Midway.

The direction of the war in the Pacific Ocean would soon be decided. But why at Midway? What was so special about the island that Japan and the United States would risk the best of their fleets in a battle around its shores?

Midway was a speck of land smack in the middle of the Pacific Ocean. Its name said it all. The island sat midway between Tokyo, Japan, and San Francisco, California.

Though small, the island was very important. The American Navy used Midway as a forward operating base. An airstrip allowed scout planes to patrol much of the central Pacific Ocean. The Japanese Navy had slipped past the island to hit Pearl Harbor, but now the Americans were on high alert.

After the Doolittle Raid, Yamamoto planned to send the Imperial Japanese fleet against Midway to capture the island and its airport. If the Japanese took Midway, they could turn the base to their advantage. They could send up their own planes to scout for US counterattacks or use the island to prepare for a possible invasion of the Hawaiian Islands.

Yamamoto also had another idea in mind when he targeted Midway. He believed that a Japanese attack on the island would force the US Navy, now reduced to relying on its aircraft carriers while the battleships from Pearl Harbor were repaired, to come out to fight.

The Japanese admiral hoped to use the attack on Midway not only to seize the island but also to destroy the American carrier fleet that had bombed Tokyo and halted a Japanese advance in the southern Pacific in the Battle of Coral Sea. If the American carriers arrived as he expected, Yamamoto planned to sink them all.

What was supposed to be a huge trap set by the Japanese now became a huge trap set by the Americans as Nimitz responded to what the US codebreakers relayed to him. He knew how many ships he faced, when they would strike, and their battle orders. Four Japanese carriers were headed to Midway to attack on June 4, 1942. Nimitz gathered the *USS Enterprise*, *USS Hornet*, and *USS Yorktown* in an effort to surprise the Japanese fleet.

The Japanese fleet arrived at Midway and launched bombers to pound the island into submission in preparation for a landing by Japanese troops. As the Japanese carriers undertook the air raid, the American carriers launched torpedo planes and dive bombers to hunt for the enemy ships.

While Yamamoto had hoped to bring out the US carriers to destroy them, he had not expected them to already be in the area. He planned to capture the island and have the airstrip ready before the American fleet showed up.

At a key moment, luck intervened.

A wave of US torpedo planes found the Japanese carriers and moved into position. Many were shot down. Several of the torpedoes were duds. The assault failed. But the attack wave drew away the Japanese fighters protecting the carrier fleet. The fighters flew off to hunt down the surviving US torpedo planes.

In the meantime, a wave of Japanese bombers had completed their run over Midway and returned to their carriers to reload. As the deck crews refueled the planes and attached explosives, reports arrived from Japanese scout planes that the US carriers had been found. The Japanese commanders immediately ordered that the crews rearm the planes with torpedoes to hit the US carriers instead of bombs to attack the island's defenses.

In that window of a few minutes, a group of American dive bombers spied the Japanese carriers through the cloud cover and plunged downward. The decks of the flattops were crowded with bombs and torpedoes. Hoses gushing with high-octane gasoline twisted across the decks and into planes with near-full tanks.

When the US dive bombers released their explosives, the Japanese carriers erupted into huge fireballs. Within minutes, three carriers were destroyed.

The lone surviving carrier quickly launched a counterattack that followed the US dive bombers back to the American fleet. Japanese bombers and torpedo planes crippled the *USS Yorktown*.

But by the end of the day, planes from the two remaining US carriers hunted down the last surviving Japanese flattop.

The Battle of Midway was over. Four of the best Japanese carriers sank with over 3,000 sailors killed, 340 aircraft destroyed, and several other ships lost or damaged. The United States lost the *USS Yorktown* and over 300 sailors were killed along with around 150 aircraft destroyed.

Despite the sacrifice, the Americans had achieved an incredible victory. Adm. Nimitz's plan had worked far better than he could have hoped. On June 4, 1942, the United States seized the initiative. It was now time for the Americans to begin pushing the Imperial Japanese forces back.

Although the Imperial Japanese Navy remained a powerful force, the four carriers lost at Midway were difficult to replace. Japan simply did not have the resources to build new carriers at a rapid pace. On the other hand, the United States was quickly mobilizing its industries to produce the ships needed to crush Japan, as Yamamoto had feared.

Yamamoto's plan to destroy the US carriers ended in disaster. He would never finish the job he started at Pearl Harbor - the destruction of the US Pacific fleet.

The American codebreakers weren't done. Within a year, they would ensure that Yamamoto, the most brilliant and experienced Japanese naval commander, was dead.

American codebreakers tracked the movements of Yamamoto from intercepts of Japanese communications. The admiral was attempting to boost morale within the military after a string of defeats as 1942 turned into 1943. American intelligence officers learned the exact arrival and departure times for one leg of Yamamoto's tour along with the locations he would visit. Plotting the admiral's flight path, the Americans decided to kill Yamamoto. They called the plan Operation Vengeance.

On April 18, 1943, a group of P-38 Lightnings took off to intercept Yamamoto's plane near a place called Bougainville in Papua New Guinea. The 18 planes flew low, barely above the waves, to avoid detection. The entire operation would take them over a thousand miles in sweltering heat. Right on schedule, they encountered Yamamoto's plane and opened up with machine guns. An engine on the plane carrying Yamamoto spewed black smoke and crashed into a jungle.

The brilliant Japanese admiral was dead. Bullets hitting the aircraft had killed him before the plane crashed. A Japanese rescue mission found his plane deep in the jungle the next day.

Japanese officials understood that news of Yamamoto's death would be a hard blow to the morale of the military and the public. For over a month, the Japanese military kept his death quiet as they prepared for the shocking announcement.

The US had won revenge for Pearl Harbor. But the Americans still needed to win the war.

Did You Know . . .

- Midway is the westernmost island of the Hawaiian Island chain. It is also the only island in that chain not part of the State of Hawaii.

- The Battle of the Coral Sea was the first time in history that two fleets fought each other without being in visual range. The entire battle was fought by aircraft launched from carriers.

- The United States Navy developed the first radar detection system in 1938. US carriers used radar to detect incoming attack planes from a long distance. The Japanese Navy lacked radar at Midway and instead relied on human lookouts. This gave the American pilots the advantage of surprise.

- Hollywood filmmaker John Ford won four best director Oscars at the Academy Awards, including for the Dust Bowl saga *The Grapes of Wrath* in 1940. Ford was at Midway to film the sailors stationed on the island when the Japanese attacked. He was wounded. His documentary *The Battle of Midway* won an Oscar in 1942.

- Chester Nimitz's grandfather was a German merchant sailor who immigrated to Fredericksburg, Texas, in the late 1840s. He built the Nimitz Hotel. Locals called it the Steamboat Hotel because of its design. Today, the hotel has been converted into The National Museum of the Pacific War to honor Adm. Chester Nimitz, who was born in Fredericksburg in 1885.

- To learn if Midway was Yamamoto's target, US codebreakers in Hawaii told the commander at Midway to broadcast over the radio that the island was running low on water. These instructions arrived at Midway through an underwater cable the Japanese could not intercept. When the Japanese relayed information about the faked water shortage using their codename for Midway, US intelligence confirmed Yamamoto's attack plans.

JAPANESE INTERNMENT

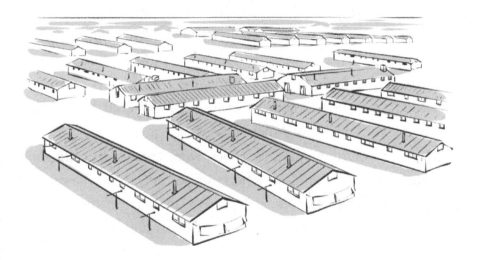

George Takei was five years old when a group of American soldiers approached the door of his family home in Los Angeles, California, in early 1942. He remembered the moment for the rest of his life: "They stopped on the front porch and with their fists they banged on the door. My father answered the door and they pointed those bayonets at all of us and told us to leave."

Takei and his family were forced from their house and placed in a horse stall at a nearby location. Soon, they were told to board a train that deposited the family behind barbed wire in a compound at Rohwer, Arkansas. Takei recalled "stern-looking soldiers glaring down at us" from platforms high above the site.

The family was eventually moved again, to a camp called the Tule Lake War Relocation Center in northern California, the largest internment site for Japanese Americans operated by the United States government. Some 18,000 lived in that Center.

Japanese Americans all along the western coast of the United States shared the Takei family's experience.

The internment of Japanese Americans resulted from Executive Order 9066, signed by President Roosevelt on February 19, 1942. The Order responded to fears that people of Japanese ancestry, even if they were US citizens, could be potential spies or saboteurs working for Imperial Japan. Race defined loyalty in many Americans' eyes.

Under the Order, military zones were created in California, Oregon, and Washington where important naval bases and factories operated. People of Japanese ancestry in these zones, especially the one closest to the coastline, had to leave. Over 120,000 Japanese-Americans were forced to live in internment camps. Nearly 80,000 of these people were US citizens. All they could take with them were a few suitcases of clothes and whatever other items they held dear.

Officially called "relocation centers," the camps took Japanese-Americans far from their lives and careers to an existence behind barbed wire guarded by armed soldiers. The 10 internment camps were in remote, desolate locations scattered across California, Idaho, Utah, Wyoming, Arizona, Colorado, and Arkansas.

On arrival at the camps, each person took a loyalty test. Their answers on the exam determined their futures. Those considered questionable in their support of the United States over Japan were concentrated at the Tule Lake, California, a high-security camp for those who resisted the relocation policy.

Inside the camps, the families were housed in military-style barracks with no insulation. A few cots were provided for beds. Privacy was minimal. Four to seven families lived in each barracks. They ate meals in mess halls. They shared bathrooms. The sites were often dusty and hot in the summer, then cold in the winter - not at all like the more stable, balmy climate of the West Coast. Most of the families forced to relocate remained in the camps until the end of the war.

The Japanese-Americans tried as hard as possible to return to some sense of normalcy. They organized schools for their children with the government's assistance. They held dances, created musical bands, or organized sports teams for entertainment. They established churches and newspapers. Some even farmed the harsh soil. For three long years, Japanese Americans were forced to make do with their situation. Only a select few thousand were allowed to leave the camps to attend college.

For some young men, however, the United States government offered an opportunity to escape the tall fences surrounding them in return for military service. Rather than turn their back on the country that had punished them for nothing other than their Japanese ancestry, thousands of Japanese Americans answered the call. They signed up to fight in the war.

The 442 Regimental Combat Team, formed in April 1943, recruited primarily second-generation Japanese Americans. Some 4,000 men, most from Hawaii but a third from internment camps, initially enlisted. They wanted to prove to the United States that they deserved respect. Overall, including replacements, about 10,000 Japanese Americans fought in the historic regiment by the end of WWII.

Reluctant to test their loyalty against the Imperial Japanese, US commanders sent the 442 Infantry Combat Team to Italy and, later, France. Often fighting in mountainous terrain, the Team earned a reputation for being among the toughest fighters in the American Army.

Although officials in Imperial Japan turned the internment of Japanese Americans into propaganda, the United States remained committed to internment until late in the war. The racist injustice of the camps boosted Imperial Japan's effort to spread propaganda that it was liberating the Pacific from the influence of White Westerners. But such attempts to win support from the Asian peoples of the Pacific often failed in light of Japanese brutality toward other Asian nations.

Several legal cases brought by Japanese Americans challenged the legality of the internment camps under the United States Constitution. By the time the cases worked through the legal system to the highest court, WWII was nearing its end.

The US Supreme Court issued a ruling forbidding the detention of American citizens without cause in December 1944. Aware that the decision was coming, President Roosevelt acted the day before the Court announced its ruling. He rescinded Order 9066 and declared that Japanese Americans in the internment camps could return home in the new year. They received $25 and a train ticket to their former residence.

Japanese Americans left the camps and tried to reestablish their lives. They struggled for years. But they were free again.

The last internment camp closed in March 1946.

Did You Know . . .

- George Takei became an actor and outspoken activist for equal rights, regardless of race or gender. In his most famous role, he played pilot Hikaru Sulu on the hit television show *Star Trek* from 1966 until 1968. Aboard the spaceship *USS Enterprise*, Takei's Sulu provided one of the first positive depictions of an Asian American in a serious television role.

- The 442 Regimental Combat Team was the most decorated unit in the US military during WWII. The Team received 4,000 Purple Hearts; a type of medal awarded to individual soldiers wounded in combat. These troops also earned 21 Congressional Medals of Honor, 29 Distinguished Service Crosses, 588 Silver Stars, and over 4,000 Bronze Stars. The Team's motto was "Go for Broke."

- Fred Korematsu refused to relocate, suing the government. His case reached the US Supreme Court. He lost but continued to fight for civil rights until he died in 2005. He received the Presidential Medal of Freedom from President Bill Clinton in 1998. Six states now celebrate Fred Korematsu Day of Civil Liberties and the Constitution each January 30.

- Daniel Inouye, born in Hawaii in 1924 to Japanese parents, enlisted in the 442 Regimental Combat Team. In 1945, while assaulting several machine gun nests, he lost his right arm to a grenade blast. He survived. In 1959, he became the first US Representative in Congress from Hawaii. He represented Hawaii in the US Senate from 1963 until he died in 2012.

- Yoshiko Uchida was born to Japanese parents in California in 1921. They were transported to the camp in Topaz, Utah. Later, she became a pioneering author of children's literature, drawing heavily from her wartime experiences. Her *Journey to Topaz: A Story of the Japanese-American Evacuation*, published in 1971, was the first book about the internment camps written by a Japanese American.
- In 1988, President Ronald Reagan signed the Civil Liberties Act. The Act granted $20,000 to each surviving internee for the US government's violation of Japanese Americans' rights during WWII. The Act noted that internment was "motivated by racial prejudice, wartime hysteria, and a failure of political leadership" and stated that "Congress apologizes on behalf of the Nation."

ROSIE THE RIVETER

"Anybody can build bombers - if we could," joked a 20-something schoolteacher named Constance Bowman Reid who taught English until WWII erupted. She laughed, "we were the kind of girls who knew nothing about airplanes except that they had wings and they flew." But, as she said, that was the aircraft industry's problem.

Factories needed workers. As in Bowman's case, employers appealed to young women working as schoolteachers to spend their summer vacations riveting ships, constructing planes, or doing some other job for the American war machine. Women felt a duty to help however they could as their men suffered and died overseas.

In the aircraft industry alone, 310,000 women by 1943 took employment in factories building planes. They accounted for nearly 65% of the workforce in that industry. Before WWII, they made up less than 1% of the aviation workforce.

The departure of men into the military opened American society to women like never before.

Roughly 10% of the US population of 132 million in 1940 joined the military. This included 37% of the male population. By 1945, some 8.2 million men served in the US Army; 3.3 million men joined the US Navy; 474,000 men served in the US Marines; and 85,000 men enlisted in the US Coast Guard. The vast majority of these enlistees ranged in age from their late teens through their forties, the prime age for industrial employment.

Women filled the jobs that men left behind, entering the workforce in unprecedented numbers. Women gained income and shifted American culture toward women's interests. To appeal to women flush with cash from their jobs, for instance, musicians started wearing colorful costumes heavy with sequins and rhinestones.

Overall, the American workforce shifted from 27% female to nearly 37% female. But the increase came less from traditional jobs worked by women, like schoolteachers and telephone operators, and more from jobs long considered reserved for men, like welding.

Attitudes toward women in the workforce became more accepting. More importantly, American society recognized more fully what women could accomplish. During the war, more than six million women accepted jobs in factories.

The gains that women made in finding employment outside the home came with anxiety over finding partners, especially men. Many young women married their boyfriends before these men enlisted. Some 73% of the men in the military were stationed overseas. The average duration of their tour of duty lasted 33 months. Many never returned. Out of every 1,000 men servicing in the military, nearly nine were killed in combat, three more died due to disease or accidents, and about 18 were wounded.

Nearly 25% of women in the workforce by 1945 were married. Rather than something strange, the idea of a wife having a job or even a career outside the home seemed normal, at least during wartime. Many of these young wives learned a new sense of independence, especially as wages were high. The idea that a woman's place was restricted to the home doing the cooking and cleaning while helping their husband became less accepted.

The reasons American women joined the war effort varied. Mary Heaton Vorse interviewed a few of the women employed at a munitions plant in Elkton, Maryland: "Ask a group of girls why they came and you get answers like this: 'I wanted to help.' 'My husband's in the Navy. I felt nearer to him, working like this.' 'My brother enlisted. I wanted to enlist too.'"

Like hundreds of other towns across the United States, the population of Elkton doubled during WWII as the nation mobilized. Often, the women employed were young, from 18-

year-olds to 20-somethings. They had grown up during the Great Depression with little money and now received fat paychecks from businesses cranking out all the stuff necessary for the US government to win the war.

Not only did a generation of women gain the opportunity to show what they could accomplish but they also gained the financial independence to pursue their own interests as never before.

All of these women became known as "Rosies" because of a magazine cover. The *Saturday Evening Post* on May 29, 1943, released an issue featuring a painting by the famed artist Norman Rockwell. The image depicted a woman in overalls employed as a riveter. The American flag waved in the background. A riveting machine, sitting across her lap, was labeled "Rosie." Her work boots pushed down on Hitler's *Mein Kampf*. The millions of women employed in war industries immediately became known by the name "Rosie the Riveter."

Some women felt uncomfortable taking jobs traditionally associated with men. Instead, they volunteered for roles considered more traditionally feminine.

American society before WWII focused on women's roles within the home as supportive wives and mothers. They cooked meals. They did the laundry. They sewed. Their responsibility meant managing the household, though they did turn some domestic chores, like laundering clothes, raising gardens, or pickling food, into ways of raising money for their families.

Around three million women volunteered for the Red Cross. These women worked as nurses, gathered pints of blood for battlefield use, and fulfilled a range of other duties within the

United States and overseas. Some worked with the Red Cross Clubmobile Service in Europe providing coffee and doughnuts to soldiers in the field, giving them comfort and a taste of home. Others drove for the Red Cross Motor Corps transporting supplies and injured soldiers.

Assisting groups like the Red Cross allowed women to stretch their domestic roles to activities outside the home. They helped wounded soldiers, sent care packages to troops in the warzone, or organized activities to boost men's morale.

Although women weren't allowed to participate in combat, the military created several affiliated organizations that supported the troops in 1942. Nearly 240,000 women served in the military.

The US Army launched the Women's Army Corps, known as the WACs. These women, numbering 150,000 during WWII, were trained in a range of specialties: switchboard operators, mechanics, cooks, typists, drivers, postal clerks, and armorers responsible for repairing firearms and other equipment. These women learned from the manual given to them on enlistment that "victory in total war will go to the side which utilizes the most women, and the fittest." Although restricted to non-combat roles, the WACs needed to prepare themselves because the "demands of war are varied, endless, and merciless."

The US Navy started the US Naval Reserve, an organization eventually called the WAVES. The name stood for Women Accepted for Volunteer Emergency Service. Doing much the same work as the WACs, WAVES numbered over 86,000 by 1945.

Military efforts related to aviation required women as well. Women interested in the new, modern world of airplanes could enlist as the Women Airforce Service Pilots, known as WASPs. Of the 25,000 that applied and roughly 1,800 that entered the flight training program, 1,074 passed. Their 57% graduation rate was better than the 50% rate of men in the military's flight training programs. These women performed tasks like test-flying aircraft, towing targets for anti-aircraft gunners, and flying cargo missions. Their service allowed men to focus on combat duties.

Most women, however, remained at home taking care of children and families. They too aided the war effort. Some helped to ration foods and other items, ensuring the military had an adequate food supply. As part of this effort, they also grew small patches of vegetables, called Victory Gardens. Women also collected tin, copper, and various metals necessary to make military equipment, from ammunition to vehicles.

Women proved essential to the American war effort. Whether at home, in the factories, or the military, all women contributed to the push toward victory.

Did You Know . . .

- Constance Bowman Reid and her friend Clara Marie Allen, a school art teacher, wrote a memoir about their summer spent building Liberator B-24 bombers in San Diego, California, in 1943. They published it as *Slacks and Calluses* a year later, one of the earliest accounts of women's participation in the war industries.

- President Roosevelt appointed Frances Perkins as Secretary of Labor when he took office in 1933. Perkins was the first woman ever appointed to a Cabinet position. Serving until June 1945, Perkins oversaw safety guidelines, minimum-wage enforcement, child labor restrictions, and other government regulations during the turmoil of the Great Depression and WWII.

- President Roosevelt's wife Eleanor was a prominent activist for human rights. She was the first 'First Lady' to hold her own press conferences at the White House. She encouraged the attendance of women journalists. She also used these press conferences to promote her programs and to encourage women's political activism.

- Norman Rockwell's model for the Rosie the Riveter cover was Mary Doyle Keefe. Keefe grew up in Vermont, where she met Rockwell, and worked as a telephone operator. She was 19 years old at the time. She never worked as a riveter.

- Grace Hopper joined the WAVES during WWII. With a PhD in mathematics, she was assigned to the Bureau of Ships Computation Project. After WWII, she continued to pioneer computer programming and the design of computer languages. In 1983, Hopper was promoted to the rank of Rear Admiral, one of the first women admirals in the US Navy.

- The Women's Armed Services Integration Act of 1948 allowed women to serve in all branches of the military. Prior to the Act, women, except for nurses, could enlist only during times of war. The Act restricted women from serving on combat ships or planes. Women finally became combat pilots in 1991 and sailed aboard warships in 1994.

DOUBLE VICTORY

A. (Asa) Philip Randolph proposed a March on Washington in January 1941. While he hadn't encountered any African Americans wanting to see the United States lose the looming war, he "found many who, before the war ends, want to see the stuffing knocked out of white supremacy and of empire over subject peoples." He stressed that African Americans were "confronted not with a choice but with a challenge both to win democracy for ourselves at home and to help win the war for democracy the world over."

Randolph's March was a threat. In 1925, he founded and become president of the Brotherhood of Sleeping Car Porters. The Brotherhood was a union of railroad workers, all of them African American. He instantly became a major figure in advancing civil rights in the United States. He knew a great deal about job discrimination based on race, and he knew that WWII had provided a chance to do something about it.

Randolph, like millions of African Americans, saw an opportunity in the outbreak of WWII. They would fight the Axis. But they also understood that the United States was hypocritical in declaring itself a defender of liberty while also denying equal rights to people of color. For African Americans, the war was the start of a longer struggle against racism, one that would start with victory overseas before being completed with a victory for equality at home after the war.

Randolph's planned March on Washington pressured President Roosevelt to end racial discrimination in the workplace. With the government spending billions on tanks, planes, artillery, and everything else needed to defeat the Axis, surely all Americans should benefit. Roosevelt could not afford the negative publicity of a racial protest in the nation's capital at a time when it was trying to stand as a defender of liberty against the racist policies of Axis countries.

Although not yet leading a country at war, Roosevelt had given a radio speech in December 1940 declaring the United States the "Arsenal of Democracy." The President intended, under the Lend-Lease Act, to send war materiel to nations fighting the Axis countries. It was this speech that now gave Randolph what he needed to turn the industrial arsenals of the

United States into guardians of freedom for everyone regardless of color.

Roosevelt responded with Executive Order 8802. The President declared that there "shall be no discrimination in the employment of workers in defense industries and in Government, because of race, creed, color, or national origin." Although restricted to factories with contracts from the federal government, the Order was a major achievement in the struggle for civil rights within the United States.

The actions taken by A. Philip Randolph and President Roosevelt against discrimination gave African Americans hope for the future. J. (Jay) Saunders Redding, an African American, at first saw little reason to join the fight as a radio broadcasted news about the Pacific into his room: "Some non-white men were killing some white men and it might be that the non-whites would win."

But as the war raged and eventually drew the United States into the conflict after Pearl Harbor, Redding, like most other African Americans, committed to fighting racism everywhere it existed. The racial views of Imperial Japan and Nazi Germany convinced American minorities of color that they had to destroy these Axis regimes. Redding explained his realization: "The ethnic theories of the Hitler 'master folk' admit of no chance of freedom, but rather glory in its expungement."

This awakening mobilized all Americans, regardless of their color. And it changed the meaning and purpose of the war. Redding explained the shift for readers of a national magazine in November 1942: "This is a war to keep men free. The struggle to broaden and lengthen the road of freedom - our own private and important war to enlarge freedom here in America - will come later."

The name given to this mobilization for civil rights at home and overseas was the Double Victory campaign. The term was coined by the *Pittsburgh Courier*, a Black-owned newspaper in Pittsburgh, Pennsylvania, in 1942. Editors for the newspaper developed the name after receiving a letter from a man asking the nationally prominent publication why he should risk his life for the war effort.

Answering the call to arms, many African Americans took employment in vital war industries left open by the departure of

White men into the military. They especially abandoned the cotton fields and other agricultural pursuits of the southern United States, where racism was worst, to seek work in factories in northern cities and urban centers along the West Coast. These jobs outside the South gave them high wartime pay and much more freedom to enjoy that wealth. This laid a foundation for the future civil rights movement.

Not that discrimination was escapable during WWII. African Americans and other minorities confronted racial violence throughout the United States.

The opportunities that were opened to African Americans during the war sparked resentment from Whites. The rapid increase of urban populations as war industries drew people together from across the countryside heightened racial tensions, especially as previously poor minorities gained decent wages if not always the best jobs, despite Roosevelt's Order 8802.

In Detroit, Michigan, the automobile industry that had cranked out so many cars by Ford, General Motors, and other manufacturers during the 1920s and 1930s now turned to making tanks, trucks, and other military vehicles. As so many White men left for the military, these factories turned to women and African Americans to fill their payrolls. The Black population of Detroit doubled during the 1940s, from 149,000 to 300,000.

In June 1943, Detroit plunged into chaos. After White and Black youths began fighting at a local amusement park, rumors of other racial clashes spread. Soon, groups of African Americans and Whites attacked each other across the city. The violence left 25 African Americans and nine Whites dead. The military rushed 3,500 soldiers to Detroit to restore peace.

Detroit was not alone. During the Summer of 1943, race-related riots broke out in Mobile, Alabama, Beaumont, Texas, and New York City.

In Los Angeles, White US sailors attacked young Mexican Americans and African Americans for wearing flashy outfits considered unpatriotic given wartime rationing. This incident became known as the Zoot Suit Riots, named for the baggy clothes the young men wore.

Despite the prejudices faced within the segregated US military, over 901,000 African Americans enlisted during WWII to advance the cause of justice and equality. They were the largest minority group in the services. According to the estimates at the time, the second largest group, with 51,000 enlisted, was of Puerto Rican ancestry, followed by Japanese Americans, with 33,000 serving, and Native Americans, with 20,000 enlisted. All experienced some form of discrimination in the largely White American society of the 1940s.

The Tuskegee Airmen became one of the most famous African American units during WWII. The Airmen were formed as an all-Black crew of combat pilots with the support of First Lady Eleanor Roosevelt, an advocate for civil rights.

Several hundred African Americans trained as pilots in Tuskegee, Alabama, home to a well-known historically Black university. At first, they received second-hand fighters when deployed to North Africa and later Italy. White military leaders doubted the Airmen's abilities.

By 1944, the Tuskegee Airmen had proven their valor in combat and received state-of-the-art P-51 Mustangs. They painted the tails of the planes red, gaining the nickname "Red

Tails." Their task was to escort US bombers to targets over Germany, taking on enemy fighters. German fighters were only able to shoot down around 25 Allied bombers protected by the Tuskegee Airmen, far fewer than the 46 bombers averaged by the other escort groups.

Equally famous were tank units operated by African Americans. The 761st Tank Battalion became the first African American tank unit to see combat in WWII. Nicknamed the "Black Panthers" with the unit motto "Come Out Fighting," they landed in France in October 1944.

One of the unit's officers, however, didn't make the trip. Lieutenant Jack Robinson had been court-martialed for refusing to move to the back of a segregated bus. Although later acquitted, the war was over before he was cleared. Jackie Robinson later became the first African American to play Major League Baseball when he suited up for the Brooklyn Dodgers in 1947.

The men of the 761st Tank Battalion saw nearly continuous heavy fighting across France and into Germany. Their army commander, General George S. Patton, complimented these tankers: "I would never have asked for you if you weren't good. I have nothing but the best in my Army."

Although a few African Americans distinguished themselves in combat, most often they found themselves doing support roles like cooking, driving, or loading and unloading supplies in the segregated military. Their work was essential to the American war machine.

African American women too joined the military to help win the war. About 6,500 Black women enlisted in the Women's Army Corps.

The 6,888th Central Postal Directory Battalion especially distinguished itself. This unit's work demonstrated how vital support roles were for the war effort.

During the war, over 3.3 billion pieces of mail journeyed through the military postal service. Mail was key to maintaining morale among the soldiers at the front. They needed news from family, friends, wives, and girlfriends to stay focused on the fight and what they were fighting for. A serious backlog in mail depressed the soldiers.

To fix the backlog in the European Theater, the army turned to the 850 Black women of the 6,888th commanded by Major Charity Adams. The battalion became the only all-African American women's US Army unit stationed overseas in WWII when they were ordered to a mail processing center in England and, later, France.

Sorting 65,000 pieces of mail every eight-hour shift, the women fixed the backlog in half the time expected. Adams was promoted to lieutenant colonel at the end of the war, making her the highest-ranking African American woman in WWII.

With the end of WWII, African Americans had demonstrated their courage and learned the toughness that comes from soldiering. WWII veteran Medgar Evers, head of the Mississippi branch of the National Association for the Advancement of Colored People after the war, later stated, "I'm looking to be shot any time I step out of my car. If I die, it will be for a good cause." Evers's efforts to integrate Mississippi and ensure African Americans' voting rights made him a target. A white supremacist assassinated him in 1963.

The surrender of the Axis ended the first half of the Double Victory campaign. The second half would continue the bloody struggle for freedom and equality, but within the United States. That struggle ended with the Civil Rights Act of 1964 and the Voting Rights Act of 1965, though the fight against racial injustice continues.

Did You Know . . .

- The Associated Negro Press was founded in Chicago in 1919. The organization linked newspapers serving African Americans in US cities with Black journalists reporting news of interest often ignored by White reporters, such as racial discrimination in factories and the military during WWII. By linking Black Americans, the agency, active until 1964, helped inspire the Civil Rights Movement.

- Aboard the *USS West Virginia*, Dorie Miller worked in the mess hall as a cook. During the attack on Pearl Harbor, he rescued the wounded and then began firing an antiaircraft gun, for which he had no training. Miller became a national hero. He died in 1943 when a Japanese torpedo sank his ship.

- In 1940, Benjamin O. Davis, Sr., became the first African American promoted to the rank of general in the US military. He had served in the US Army since the Spanish-American War in 1898, often facing discrimination within the racially segregated military. His son, Benjamin O Davis, Jr., served with the Tuskegee Airmen. In 1954, Davis, Jr., became the first African American promoted to general in the US Air Force.

- Born in St. Louis, Missouri, in 1906, Josephine Baker left the United States for more racially liberal Paris, France. Her dancing and singing made her famous during the 1920s and 1930s. She joined the French Resistance during WWII, spying on Nazi officials. Baker later received the Croix de Guerre and Legion of Honor, France's highest military and civilian awards.

- President Harry Truman issued Executive Order 9981 in July 1948. The Order abolished discrimination based on race, religion, or national origin in all branches of the military. The US Air Force, established as an independent branch of the military in September 1947, was the first part of the American military to integrate fully.

- The United States Supreme Court ordered the end of segregation in its *Brown v Board of Education of Topeka* decision in 1954. The case looked at racially segregated schools. The Justices ruled that "separate education facilities are inherently unequal." Their decision became the legal basis for eliminating all laws supporting segregation in the United States.

ISLAND-HOPPING

Richard Tregaskis worked with the US Marines clearing the island of Guadalcanal. For six months, from August 1942 until February 1943, the US Marines and US Army fought a vicious battle to force out the Imperial Japanese troops. It was the first leap taken by American troops during an island-hopping campaign aimed straight at Imperial Japan.

The combat observed by Tregaskis was vicious. The Japanese "had dug innumerable large caves into the limestone walls of the ravine, and from the narrow mouths of these dugouts they fired rifles, automatic rifles and machine guns." US soldiers crawled close and tossed dynamite at and, finally, into the enemy strongholds. Day after day, the Americans inched forward.

Death haunted every step. "Everywhere one turned there were piles of bodies." Tregaskis detailed the various ways brave men had died, with the dead scattered among shattered rocks and equipment and spent ammunition shells. But what haunted Tregaskis were the bodies "bloated like overstuffed sausages" decaying in the heat of the South Pacific!

All the deaths should have shocked me. And it did, but only briefly. Tregaskis explained, "there is no horror to these things. The first one you see is the only shock. The rest are simple repetition."

Richard Tregaskis published his observations of combat as *Guadalcanal Diary* in 1943, a book that became a bestseller and quickly made it into a Hollywood hit movie. Although the film avoided the gore of combat, the book hit hard. What Americans read brought the realities of war home. Those realities also shaped the military's approach to defeating Imperial Japan and ending the war with victory.

At Guadalcanal, American troops, joined by a few units mostly from the United Kingdom, New Zealand, and Australia, fought their first pitched battle against Japanese soldiers. The campaign to take the island was also the first step in the Allied shift to fighting a long offensive to push back the Japanese forces.

News that the Japanese were constructing an airfield on Guadalcanal made an assault on the island urgent. If the Japanese completed the airfield, their long-range planes could hit Allied ships sailing between the United States and Australia. At the same time, to draw away Japanese reinforcements, US Gen. MacArthur led an offensive through New Guinea on his way to the Philippines.

The campaign to take Guadalcanal involved over 60,000 Allies, mostly Americans, against more than 36,000 Japanese. Of these, the Allies lost around 7,100 dead and the Japanese lost 19,200 dead.

Americans encountered the fierce fighting style of Japanese soldiers. This included the banzai charge, a suicidal wave of yelling men running in an attack formation. Their charge tried to overwhelm and panic the American troops. Rather than surrender to the Allies, Japanese soldiers chose to kill themselves before dishonoring their emperor by being defeated. The deaths shocked the American military.

After winning control of Guadalcanal, the Americans focused on taking another island named Tarawa. This speck of land, barely 12 square miles, contained an airfield that gave the Imperial Japanese the ability to scout much of the middle of the Pacific Ocean. Removing the outpost would free the Allies to strike deep into territory held by Imperial Japan.

The US Marines, numbering 18,000 men, landed on Tarawa for a brutal four-day battle in November 1943. The 4,500 Japanese soldiers put up stiff resistance.

Beach landings, as at Tarawa, often involved tough fighting. US soldiers were forced to wade through water and then run across a barren beach before finding cover from enemy fire. Robert Sherrod wrote of the landing zones at Tarawa: "Fifty feet further up the beach, ten Marines were killed on the barbed wire on the coral flats. One of them was evidently shot as he placed his foot on the top rung of the wire - his trouser leg was caught on the barbs and the leg still hangs in the air. There are eighty more dead Marines scattered in a twenty-foot square of the beach just beyond."

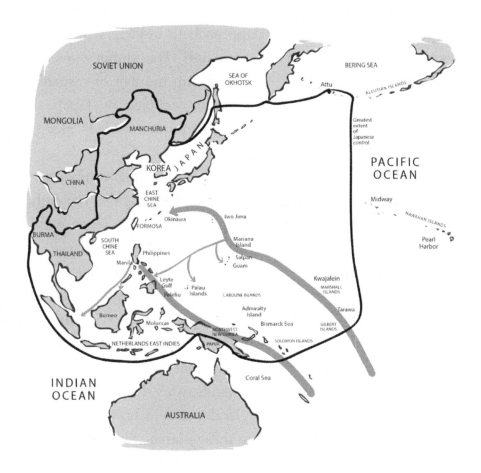

Once they established a beachhead, the US Marines faced well-prepared Imperial Japanese units. Snipers sat in palm trees. Machine gun nests lay hidden in underground bunkers. For over a year, the Japanese had fortified the island as part of Yamamoto's plan to make the war as bloody as possible for the Americans in hopes of wearing down their will to fight.

At the end of the intense battle, the US Marines had suffered more than 1,000 killed and 2,000 wounded. All of the Japanese troops were dead except for 17 captured soldiers.

The deadly fight for such a small piece of territory convinced Adm. Chester Nimitz and other Allied commanders in the Pacific Theater that the best approach to quickly winning the war was an island-hopping campaign. The strategy avoided Yamamoto's plan to inflict the maximum number of casualties. Instead of conquering all the islands occupied by Japan, the Allies would only target the most important islands along a route straight toward Japan.

Under the island-hopping strategy, the Americans minimized casualties by only risking landings on key islands. The fights would still be bloody. But this approach to defeat Japan would be far less costly to lives and bodies.

As for the islands left under Japanese control, the Allied fleets would cut off their supplies. The Allied Fleet Navies basically placed these Imperial Japanese forces under siege. The ultimate goal was to attack mainland Japan, forcing a surrender of the government and military leadership that would then convince the Japanese troops on outlying islands to lay down their arms.

In 1944, the American Navy landed troops on the islands of Guam, Tinian, and Saipan. From these islands, the United States could launch long-range bombers to strike targets like shipyards, military camps, and factories on mainland Japan.

American soldiers also conquered Peleliu and Angaur. These two islands provided airstrips for bombing raids on the Philippines.

The campaign to capture these islands, along with a few others, involved around 128,000 Allied troops. Some 8,100 were killed in the fighting. The Japanese forces numbered about 71,000. Over 67,000 of these soldiers died.

Tom Lea, a war correspondent with the 1st Marine Division, described the heart-pounding experience of making the landings on a beach like Peleliu. When the front of the landing craft dropped onto the sand, the men inside became vulnerable to enemy fire. Everyone aboard scrambled for cover: "Each man drew into himself when he ran down that ramp, into that flame. Those marines flattened in the sand on that beach were dark and huddled like wet rats in death as I threw my body down among them."

The rattle and roar of battle, the smell of burning oil and spent gunpowder, and the sight of wounded men shredded by shrapnel terrified me. But the American troops pressed on, capturing island after island.

In October 1944, Gen. Douglas MacArthur returned to the Philippines. Until the end of the war in August 1945, a US army of over a million soldiers fought a Japanese army of 529,000 men.

The US military on the path to Japan next targeted Iwo Jima. American commanders wanted the island as an airfield where fighter planes could be based. Fighter planes had a shorter range than bombers. The island, being closer to Japan, would allow US fighters to escort bombers during their raids on Japan's home island.

For five weeks from February through March 1945, the United States sent 70,000 US Marines to capture Iwo Jima from the 18,000 Imperial Japanese soldiers defending it. Iwo Jima's defining feature was Mount Suribachi, a mountain towering 550 feet above the island. The Japanese maintained a network of artillery and machine gun nests connected by tunnels and bunkers. When US Marines raised the American flag on Mount Suribachi, Joe Rosenthal snapped a photograph of the event. The image of the US Marines became an iconic symbol of the war effort.

The well-fortified island cost the lives of nearly 7,000 Americans with another 20,000 wounded. The US Marines only captured 216 Japanese soldiers, the rest fighting to the death.

With the fall of Iwo Jima, the United States prepared to take the war into its final phase - an invasion of the home islands of Japan. The final target of the island-hopping campaign was Okinawa, an island large enough and close enough to mainland Japan to serve as a staging area for the Allied militaries.

Did You Know . . .

- Tarawa is now home to 56,000 people. The population density stands at 5,261 people per square mile. In the 1940s, the island contained a population of 1,641. Tarawa today is one of the most crowded islands in the Pacific Ocean. Tarawa forms part of the Republic of Kiribati, which gained independence from the United Kingdom in 1979.

- Attu is the western-most island of Alaska's Aleutian Islands. It was captured by the Japanese in June 1942 to establish an airfield to patrol the northern Pacific Ocean. In May 1943, US troops along with Canadian units liberated Attu. It was the only battle between the US and Japan fought in snowy conditions.

- George Bush, Sr., became a naval combat pilot at 18 years old. Japanese anti-aircraft guns downed Bush's TBM Avenger over the island Chi An gaur Jima in September 1944. Bush bailed out with another man, but that man's parachute didn't open. The submarine *USS Finback* rescued Bush from the Pacific Ocean four hours later. Bush served as US President from 1989 until 1993.

- The islands in the Pacific Ocean were often formed of volcanic rock and ash that bubbled up from the ocean floor. The rock and ash made digging into the ground to create protection from enemy fire very difficult. Worse, the volcanic rock tended to shatter if hit by mortars or artillery shells, adding to the dangers of combat.

- US Marines raised a small American flag on Mount Suribachi during the Battle of Iwo Jima. Military commanders soon ordered it replaced with a larger American flag, one more visible to soldiers fighting across the island. This flag-raising was photographed by Joe Rosenthal. Three of the six US Marines photographed died in combat during the next few days.

- Mexico declared war on the Axis nations on May 28, 1942, after German submarines sank oil tankers in Mexico's territorial waters. Mexico's 201st Fighter Squadron nicknamed the Aztec Eagles, consisted of nearly 300 personnel. The unit served in the Philippines starting in February 1945, the only military unit in Mexican history to engage in combat outside of Mexico.

STALINGRAD

As the Americans and their Allies slugged it out with the Imperial Japanese forces on volcanic islands and in the thick jungles of the Pacific Theater, the war in the European Theater largely centered on a brawl between Nazi Germany and the Soviet Union.

After occupying France in June 1940, the German military established airfields and submarine bases along the coast of western European to target the United Kingdom. Bombing raids by the Luftwaffe pummeled British industry and frightened the population. The Battle of Britain involved the Royal Air Force of the United Kingdom trying to hold off these attacks and any possible German invasion.

Meanwhile, German submarines working in groups known as wolfpacks attacked Allied ships headed to the United Kingdom with supplies. The Battle of the Atlantic was underway as the warships of the Allies hunted the submarines.

The war stalemated around the United Kingdom. The British Navy was too strong for the Germans to launch a successful invasion and the British ground forces were too weak to push the Nazis out of France.

By the end of 1940, Hitler looked to conquer the Soviet Union despite having signed a non-aggression pact with Stalin the previous year. His military began work on Operation Barbarossa, a planned full-scale offensive to destroy the Soviet Union within a few weeks. Blitzkrieg had worked so successfully against the modern militaries of western European countries that the German high command believed the weaker Russian military, though massive in numbers, would be easily defeated.

In June 1941, Nazi Germany launched a wave of over three million soldiers, some 3,500 tanks, 7,000 artillery pieces, and 2,500 combat aircraft into the Soviet Union. The invasion force was the largest in human history. The battlefront stretched for 1,800 miles. They overwhelmed the poorly-trained three million troops of the Soviet Union's Red Army armed and equipped with 11,000 tanks and thousands of outdated aircraft.

War correspondent Larry LeSueur observed the tattered Soviet ranks as the German offensive relentlessly pushed them back toward Moscow in late 1941. He "passed an entire brigade of Red Army men who looked as though they had been marching for days. Their faces were black with fatigue. They were dragging their feet in exhaustion." In the distance, a heavy rumble of artillery shook the ground and the men. LeSueur continued, "Several times we saw men stumble as they plodded forward and fall unconscious on the snow. The columns never stopped moving, but I saw fellow soldiers pick up their companions and place them, senseless, on passing sleds which were loaded with hay."

By December 1941, the German military was on the outskirts of Moscow and Leningrad, known today as St. Petersburg.

Then, the Russians under General Georgy Zhukov counterattacked, pushing the Germans back.

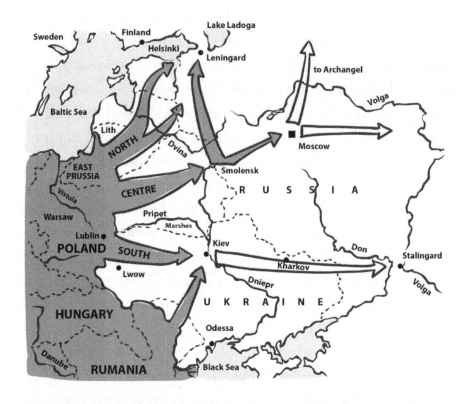

During 1942, the German military focused on laying siege to
Leningrad at the north end of the front and capturing Stalingrad
at the south end. Both had symbolic significance. Leningrad was
named for Vladimir Lenin, the founder of the Soviet Union. The
city was the cultural center of Russia and the place where the
Russian Revolution erupted in 1917.

Stalingrad was named for the Soviet leader in power, Joseph
Stalin. The city served as a gateway to the oilfields south of the
city in the Caucasus Mountains. Nazi Germany desperately
needed access to those oil wells to fuel their modern war
machine of mechanized infantry, tanks, and planes.

Stalin refused to evacuate civilians from either Leningrad or Stalingrad. He believed the Red Army would fight harder with people living in the cities.

The battle for Leningrad became a siege lasting for 872 days from September 1941 until January 1944. Around 650,000 civilians died from either starvation, exposure to the cold, disease, or shelling from the German guns.

The five-month battle for Stalingrad raged from August 1942 until February 1943. The German army, known as the Wehrmacht, hammered the Red Army in fierce street-fighting. In close combat, moving from room to room across the city, the two armies battled. The freezing Russian winter made conditions even worse.

Located on the Volga River, the Red Army was pinned against the shoreline. To keep a foothold in Stalingrad, Soviet military leaders poured reinforcements across the river, often under heavy German artillery fire and strafing attacks by planes. The combat was so intense that the average life expectancy of a Soviet soldier in Stalingrad was 24 hours.

Eventually, a Soviet counteroffensive cut off the supply line to the German Army in Stalingrad. The German soldiers were trapped.

By the end of the battle, over 800,000 Germans were casualties. The Soviets lost 1.1 million casualties. But the Red Army had held. The Soviet Union with its large population could more easily replace the soldiers lost than Germany could.

Defeated at Stalingrad, the German military reeled as the Red Army pushed the Nazi invaders back.

To regain the initiative, the German commanders charged the Soviets during the Battle of Kursk from July to August 1943. The Nazis gathered 780,000 soldiers, 3,000 tanks, and 2,000 aircraft. But the Red Army countered with 1.9 million troops, 5,000 tanks, and 3,000 aircraft. Kursk became famous for featuring the largest tank battle in history. Despite furious assaults by the Germans, the Soviets won.

After the Battle of Kursk, the German military could no longer organize large offensives on the Eastern Front. The losses in men and equipment had been too great.

The Nazis could now only delay a relentless Soviet offensive rolling straight to Germany's capital, Berlin.

Did You Know . . .

- Operation Barbarossa was named for Frederick Barbarossa, a man who became a powerful leader of the Holy Roman Empire during the 1100s CE. Barbarossa reigned under the title of Emperor Frederick I. The Empire had contained much of what became Nazi Germany. The reference to Frederick Barbarossa highlighted the Nazi fascination with legendary German leaders of the past.

- Adolf Hitler proclaimed that the Nazis had established the Third Reich, an empire he promised would last 1,000 years. It only survived 12 years. The First Reich referred to the Holy Roman Empire, which existed from 800 CE to 1806 CE. The Second Reich lasted from Germany's unification in 1871 until the end of WWI in 1918.

- Hitler imagined himself a great military leader. To be closer to fighting on the Eastern Front against the Soviet Union, he built a concrete command center called the Wolf's Lair, located in present-day Poland. On July 20, 1944, Col. Claus von Stauffenberg attempted to assassinate Hitler with a bomb as part of a coup. Hitler survived.

- Gen. Friedrich Paulus commanded the German 6th Army at Stalingrad. After being cut off and surrounded, Paulus surrendered the Army. Hitler promoted him to field marshal, expecting Paulus to die rather than be captured. But Paulus refused. In Soviet hands, he became a loud critic of Hitler and aided Soviet efforts to win support in eastern Europe.

- The 1077th Anti-Aircraft Regiment was the first Soviet unit to fire upon the Nazi German Army as it arrived at Stalingrad. The unit contained many teenage women barely out of high school who volunteered to serve despite having no combat experience. They held off the Germans for two days.
- Vasily Zaitsev was a sniper in the Red Army. He is considered one of the best marksmen of all time. During the Battle of Stalingrad, he killed at least 225 German soldiers and officers. A mortar explosion in January 1943 injured his eyes, ending his career as an effective sniper.

AIR SUPREMACY

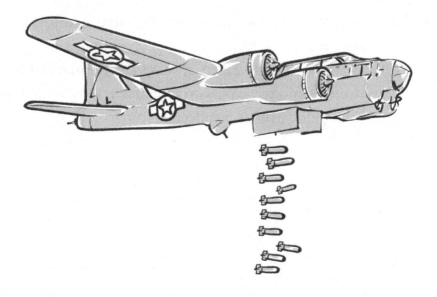

"I know there may be some who call it uncivilized warfare," explained Curtis Lemay as he developed strategies for the US air forces, "but you simply can't fight a war without some civilian casualties." Lemay believed in fighting a total war in which civilians were reasonable targets as they helped keep the enemy armies fighting. He argued, "We didn't start this war, but the quicker we finish it, the more lives we will save - and not just Americans. We want to avoid killing civilians, if possible, but keep in mind that the Japanese workers who manufacture weapons are part and parcel of their military machine. My first duty is to protect and save as many of our crews as possible."

Bombing campaigns over the Axis countries grew more intense with each year of the war. The longer the war dragged on, the more the Allies searched for ways to end the conflict as quickly as possible.

Beirne Lay recalled how much the air war fought by the United States changed between 1942 and 1943. He remembered watching a "pitifully small force of twelve B-17s take off on the first raid of the 8th Air Force to make a shallow penetration against Rouen, France" in August 1942. A year later he joined an attack wave numbering 360 bombers all headed deep into Nazi Germany.

As the bomber he was in crossed the German border, the first burst of flak blossomed in front of the plane. Soon, fighters from the Luftwaffe, the Nazi German air force, popped up from the ground to strafe the US bombers. "From now on we were in mortal danger," said Lay, "my mouth dried up and my buttocks pulled together." The noise was nearly unbearable. Lay sat stunned: "The guns from every B-17 in our group and the group ahead were firing simultaneously, lashing the sky with ropes of orange tracers to match the chain-puff bursts squirting from the 20-mm. cannon muzzles in the wings."

The scene seemed unreal. The bombers "flew through the cluttered wake of a desperate air battle, in which disintegrating aircraft were commonplace and the white dots of sixty parachutes in the air at one time were hardly worth a second look," Lay marveled, "the spectacle registering on my eyes became so fantastic that my brain turned numb to the actuality of the death and destruction all around us. Had it not been for the squeezing in my stomach, which was trying to purge, I might easily have been watching an animated cartoon in a movie theater."

"I knew I was going to die," recalled Lay.

But, luckily, Lay and most of the bomber crews reached their target and made it back to their airfields to rest, repair any damage, and reload for the next raid. Some 200 airmen and 24 bombers didn't make it back, almost 7% of those who had lifted off earlier that day.

The most famous air raid by the American air force occurred in October 1943. Over 250 B-17 bombers targeted the factories in Schweinfurt, Germany. Sixty bombers with 600 airmen never returned from the mission.

The losses in the air war were severe. Around 12,000 US heavy bombers alone were shot down during WWII. But the productivity of industries mobilized by the US government more than matched this loss rate. American factories rolled 276,000 aircraft off the assembly line.

The pilots and their crews were far less replaceable. It took months to train new airmen. And the experience gained from actual escort sorties or bombing runs could not be taught. Luckily for the Allies, the struggles of the Axis to replace destroyed aircraft was much tougher and the loss of airmen even harder to solve given their shortages of resources and manpower.

The American air force emphasized pinpoint bombings in the first couple of years of the war. This tactic relied on the success of the Norden Bombsight; a device created by Swiss engineer Carl Norden. The device acted as an early type of computer, adjusting for wind speed, air density, and other various factors that could alter a bomb's accuracy as it dropped from the plane.

The Allies guarded the Norden Bombsight like a secret weapon. Bombardiers took an oath to protect this equipment with their lives. Crews were instructed to destroy the Norden Bombsight if they crashed. To make this easier, the sights were loaded with thermite, a compound that when triggered melted the targeting system into a useless metal lump.

As the war proceeded into late 1944, the targeted bombing of factories gave way to carpet-bombing whole cities in order to break the will of the Axis population. Hitting the civilian population promised to exhaust the German people and erode their ability to keep armies supplied with new soldiers and goods. British Prime Minister Winston Churchill along with other Allied leaders believed a terror bombing campaign gutting urban centers would significantly disrupt the Nazi war effort. Also, the bombings would flood Germany with refugees, draining vital supplies otherwise sent to the armies and clogging the transportation network.

The British push to destroy Germany's cities stemmed from the Luftwaffe's relentless bombings of the United Kingdom. Air raids over Great Britain devastated cities. A German assault on Belfast in 1941, for example, killed over 1,000 people, hit half the houses in the city and left 100,000 homeless.

As the Allies shot down Luftwaffe bombers that Germany could not afford to replace, Hitler put into action a new technology - rockets. He tried the V-1, a crude flying bomb. But then the Nazi military invested in the V-2 rocket, a guided missile. The "V" stood for "Vengeance." Over 1,100 V-2s were built and fired at the Allies, mainly into the United Kingdom, between 1944 and 1945. The rockets killed around 5,000 people and around 10,000 enslaved laborers in concentration camps run by the Nazis died building the rockets.

The Allies responded by hammering Germany as they gained air supremacy from 1943 onward.

The Allied bombing raids stripped Axis cities bare. In Germany, the wreckage of major cities haunted the landscape. A Swiss journalist observed the widespread destruction in 1944: "In Munich, and Augsburg, Stuttgart, Darmstadt, and Frankfurt, Leipzig and Berlin. Ruins and rubble everywhere, debris and broken glass." The crumbling buildings littered the streets along with their contents - furniture, typewriters, lamps, bathtubs, sewing machines, roof tiles, and glass shards.

The people of these cities tried to maintain their routines amid shortages of food, clothes, and other necessities. Signs on the rubble heaps pointed passersby to where former residents of the destroyed homes now lived. The Swiss reporter saw other signs as well "warning 'Caution, rat poison sprayed on this site!' . . . .

For the rats in these unhappy cities can find plenty to feed on, and have become a dangerous plague." Where rats ran wild, diseases followed.

The fire-bombing of Dresden became the most infamous incident of this air raid campaign over Nazi Germany. On February 13, 1945, the British Bomber Command sent 800 bombers loaded with 2,700 tons of explosives, including large numbers of incendiaries designed to spark fires, to the city. The US 8th Air Force attacked with over 200 bombers and 400 tons of explosives the next day. Dresden, a city not yet widely bombed by the Allies, was unprepared for what happened next.

Dresden contained a population of 600,000, making it Germany's seventh-largest city. By February 1945, an additional 300,000 refugees fleeing the Red Army's advance along the Eastern Front had crowded into Dresden. The attack on the city, along with neighboring Chemnitz and Leipzig, weakened Germany's ability to resist the approaching Soviet troops.

The explosion of bombs dropped on Dresden, along with the weather conditions and the large number of flammable materials in the undamaged city, sparked a firestorm. The heat was intense. And the flames sucked the oxygen from the air. Roughly 70% of the people killed in the attack suffocated from carbon monoxide released by the fire. Estimates suggest between 25,000 to 35,000 residents died.

The effect of fire-bombings on Japanese cities proved even more destructive and deadly. Outside of industrial areas and downtowns, Japanese cities used a lot of wood. Homes often contained paper screens for room dividers and woven grass mats for flooring - all highly flammable.

Only a month after the terrifying assault on Dresden, the American military targeted Tokyo with a fire-bombing raid.

The precision bombing preferred by US aviators proved difficult over Japan. High-altitude attacks on industrial and military targets faced tough Japanese air defenses and strong jet-stream winds that worsened inaccuracies.

The military turned to Gen. Curtis Lemay to develop its new strategy. He decided to adopt techniques of the British Bomber Command.

For US commanders in the Pacific Theater, now confronting an enemy more determined than ever to avoid defeat and defend their sacred home island, gutting Japanese cities of infrastructure and people seemed a way of shortening the war.

The death of a civilian was the death of a worker powering the Imperial Japanese war machine. The loss of the very young and very elderly was seen as an ugly necessity of modern warfare.

Lemay suggested nighttime strikes at low altitudes with bombers stripped of guns and protective metal plating so that they could carry more explosives. For Tokyo, LeMay gathered a fleet of 334 bombers armed with 1,665 tons of incendiaries, including white phosphorus and napalm. He targeted an area filled with small factories.

A strike on the capital would also disrupt the government and military while sending shockwaves through the Japanese population, lowering their morale and possibly their will to fight.

The dry weather and windy conditions intensified the blaze that erupted across Tokyo as the bombers unleashed their payloads. Soon, 16 square miles of the Japanese capital disappeared in a massive fire. The heat - reaching 1,800 F - became so intense that asphalt, glass, and metal melted. All the water in swimming pools evaporated. Black ash rained down.

Though above the fire, the smoke and smell from the blaze below filled the American planes through their open bomb bays. The heat rising upward even flipped over a few US bombers flying in the later attack waves.

The bombing raid on Tokyo left a million people homeless. More than 250,000 buildings were destroyed. Around 110,000 residents of Tokyo were killed.

Within the next week, US bombers carried out similar attacks on Nagoya, Osaka, and Kobe.

After the destruction of Tokyo and other cities, the Japanese realized that the war was a doomed cause. Defeat seemed inevitable. Cities lay in rubble and essential factories that supplied the military were erased.

Yet the shame of defeat was too much for the Imperial Japanese Army and Navy to accept. They planned to fight to the death rather than surrender. So, the war in the Pacific dragged on.

Did You Know . . .

- On June 26, 1944, the Luftwaffe put in the air the first operational jet fighter, the Messerschmitt Me 262 Swallow. It engaged a British Royal Air Force reconnaissance plane flying over southern Germany. The Swallow achieved top speeds of 540 miles per hour, 100 miles per hour faster than the fastest Allied fighter called the P-51 Mustang.

- Erich Hartmann, a fighter pilot in Germany's Luftwaffe, is recognized as the world's most successful ace. He flew 825 combat sorties and recorded 352 downed Allied planes, almost all against Soviet planes along the Eastern Front. Describing his successful technique, Hartmann said, "Coming out of the sun and getting close; dog-fighting was a waste of time."

- To allow for high-altitude bombings, the aviation industry introduced the first pressurized cabin system. Without this technology, pilots and crews could not fly above 15,000 feet without wearing oxygen masks that restricted their movement. The B-29 bomber, known as the Superfortress, was the first mass-produced military aircraft equipped with a pressurized cabin.

- The United States manufactured over 276,000 aircraft during the war. From the start of 1942 until the end of the war in August 1945, the US lost 170 planes each day. Of the roughly 43,000 planes lost, some 23,000 were destroyed in combat. US planes sent overseas burned 9.7 billion gallons of gasoline, fired 459.7 billion rounds of ammunition, and dropped 7.9 million bombs.

- On September 18, 1947, the United States Air Force was established as a separate military branch. Before WWII, planes scouted enemy positions and provided close support to soldiers. Most American air power was therefore under the army's authority. The bombing campaigns of WWII showed the unique role of planes in modern warfare, reaching deep into enemy territory.

- German scientist Werner von Braun pioneered rocket development, creating the V-2 rocket as the world's first long-range guided ballistic missile. After WWII, the United States government brought von Braun to the US to develop missiles and, later, to lead the National Aeronautics and Space Administration's program to put astronauts on the moon.

OPERATION OVERLORD

Soviet leader Joseph Stalin was suspicious of the other members of the Allies, especially the United Kingdom and the United States. The victories over the Nazi military at Stalingrad and Kursk came at a high cost of lives. Stalin was eager for the other partners in the war against the Axis to increase pressure on Germany along the Western Front to force Hitler to draw troops away from the Soviet Union.

So far, much of the help the Soviet Union had received was in the form of supplies provided by the United States under the Lend-Lease Act, passed in 1941. The Act authorized President

Roosevelt to provide American-made products to countries he considered important to the safety of the United States.

The Americans shipped military hardware like planes, tanks, ships, and firearms. Allies also received from the United States chemicals, radios, and construction equipment needed to build roads and airfields. Roosevelt also provided clothing and food, including canned meat, dried beans, evaporated milk, flour, and orange juice. Over 15% of the money spent by the US government during WWII paid for supplies sent to other countries.

The Soviet Union received 23% of all US goods shipped under the Lend-Lease Act. The supplies kept the country in the fight against Nazi Germany as the Wehrmacht overran Soviet defenses in 1941 and 1942. Only the United Kingdom received a higher percentage of wartime essentials under the Act - 63% of the goods shipped abroad by the US.

But more than supplies, Stalin now wanted President Roosevelt and UK Prime Minister Winston Churchill to land troops to fight the Axis. He believed that the Americans and British were allowing the Soviets to carry the burden of fighting. Stalin thought these capitalist countries wanted Soviet communists weakened so that the capitalists could expand their influence after WWII.

However, the United States and the United Kingdom simply couldn't take on a major fight against Nazi Germany early in the conflict. During 1942 and 1943, the United States struggled to gain the upper hand over Imperial Japan in the Pacific Ocean. The United Kingdom, during those same years, fought off bombing raids and submarines sent by Germany to cripple the country. Both Allied countries were reluctant to open a major offensive against very skilled and well-equipped Axis troops until their homelands were safe.

Yet both Western Allies prepared for an eventual assault against the Nazis. Roosevelt and Churchill agreed to place command over the European Theater under the authority of US Gen. Dwight Eisenhower with assistance from British Gen. Bernard Law Montgomery.

Gen. Eisenhower was raised in Abilene, Kansas, with a strong religious background. His experience came from training troops and working in the logistics of supplying an army during WWI and during the interwar decades. His strengths as a commander came from understanding large armies and the politics of cooperation. Eisenhower was a good listener and very intelligent. He was also humble. Speaking at an event in London shortly after the war ended in Europe, Eisenhower said, "Humility must always be the portion of any man who receives acclaim earned in the blood of his followers and sacrifices of his friends."

Roosevelt and Churchill, in consultation with Eisenhower, agreed to launch their first joint offensive in North Africa rather than Europe. They called the campaign Operation Torch. The United Kingdom wanted to seize control of the Mediterranean Sea and ease pressure on its forces in Egypt, where British troops defended the Suez Canal. The Americans agreed. The Allies landed 65,000 troops along the shores of northern Africa in November 1942 along three different beachheads.

By landing in northern Africa, the United States and United Kingdom hoped to spark an uprising. Morocco, Algeria, and Tunisia were French colonies now targeted by the US and UK. When the Nazis defeated France in June 1940, the Germans took control of France's Atlantic coast but, in the southwest, allowed a puppet regime to exist called Vichy France. Vichy France held weak control over these African territories.

The United States and the United Kingdom believed that Operation Torch would also aid in establishing a firm base for Free France. After the country's defeat, some French refused to surrender to the Nazis, establishing Free France headquartered in London under Gen. Charles de Gaulle. The Free French leader would now help the US and UK in its first major offensive against the Axis powers of Europe.

Making contact with Vichy French officials along northern Africa, the Americans, British, and Free French convinced them to welcome the Allies as liberators. Eisenhower's soldiers met little resistance when they landed on the beaches. Few in the Arab population felt loyalty to Vichy France given the racist policies of the Axis. French military officers saw helping the Allies as the first step in delivering France from Nazi occupation.

The disorganized Italian military largely responsible for defending northern Africa struggled to hold off the advancing Allies. This forced the Germans to send reinforcements. But the famed Panzer Korps of tanks commanded by German Gen. Erwin Rommel had little success. The Axis powers had to withdraw from northern Africa. Those that could not escape across the waters of the Mediterranean Sea surrendered in May 1943.

The Allies had targeted northern Africa partly to chip away at Vichy France and give Free France officials a strong base of operations. After achieving victory, the Allies planned to continue prying away the weaker partners of the Axis alliance.

The Allies' next target was Italy. From July until August 1943, they invaded and conquered the Italian island of Sicily. The landings led Italian leaders to turn against Benito Mussolini. He was arrested. The new government declared an armistice with the Allies. Germany retaliated by freeing Mussolini and seizing power. Italy fractured, with some Italians helping the Nazis and others fleeing to join the Allies.

In January 1944, the Allies landed troops along the beaches of Anzio on "the boot of Italy." Some 615,000 Allied soldiers confronted over 490,000 Axis troops. Within months the Allies were approaching Rome, the Italian capital.

The fight up the Italian peninsula was vicious, especially as the largely American and British armies faced well-trained and well-equipped German units. The mountainous terrain made for slow progress. But everywhere, the Allies were welcomed as liberators.

Observing the advance, the writer John Steinbeck noted the importance of supply lines in modern warfare. He wrote, "The highways are lined with trucks full of the incredible variety of war material for the invasion of Italy. There are thousands of items necessary to a modern army and, because of the complexity of supply, a modern army is a sluggish thing."

A campaign involved incredible difficulty. Steinbeck explained, "Plans, once made, are not easily changed, for every move of combat troops is paralleled by hundreds of moves behind the lines, the moves of food, ammunition, trucks that must get there on time."

Failure in any part of this operation connecting combat troops along the frontline to the depots with food, ammo, and other equipment could bring ruin: "If the whole big, sluggish animal does not move with perfect cooperation, it is very likely that it will not move at all."

Somehow, the large American and British armies, aided by units from other nations, managed to keep advancing. In June 1944, the Allies finally captured Rome.

Although the bulk of Italy had been taken, the Allies maintained a slow advance, reaching northern Italy by April and May 1945. But the Americans and British knew that the offensive through Italy would be bottled up at the Alps, a forbidding mountain range. To liberate mainland France and invade Nazi Germany, the Allies needed to make another major amphibious assault on an Axis-occupied beach.

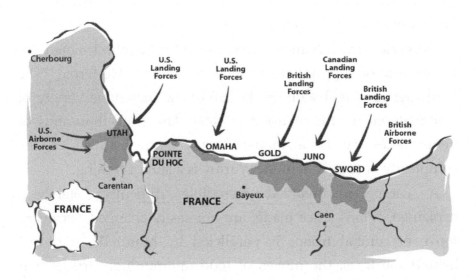

Gen. Dwight Eisenhower decided that the Allies would land along the sandy shores of Normandy in France. The military called the plan Operation Overlord. Soviet leader Joseph Stalin finally had the major Western Front offensive he had been demanding.

On June 6, 1944, Allied troops landed on five beaches codenamed Utah, Omaha, Gold, Juno, and Sword. Roughly 7,000 ships ferried almost 133,000 soldiers from 12 Allied countries into France. Despite stiff resistance from the 50,000 German defenders along the beaches, the Allied Army punched through the fortifications. The Axis and Allies lost around 10,000 casualties each.

Ernie Pyle, a war correspondent, arrived on Omaha Beach the day after the first landings. Fighting still raged in the fields beyond the beachhead. Sniper fire mixed with an occasional landmine detonation. The explosions sprayed death and sand high into the air. The shore buzzed with activity and destruction: "Submerged tanks and overturned boats and burned trucks and shell-shattered jeeps and sad little personal belongings were strewn all over these bitter sands. That plus the bodies of soldiers lying in rows covered with blankets, the toes of their shoes sticking up in line as though on a drill." Everywhere Pyle looked, he saw the chaos of battle: "And other bodies, uncollected, still sprawling grotesquely in the sand or half hidden by the high grass beyond the beach."

By the end of the month, over 850,000 men and 148,000 vehicles, including tanks, were rushing into France. In late August 1944, Paris was liberated from Nazi control. Each passing day made more of France free.

Much of the Allied success in France came with the help of the French Resistance, the secret effort by French citizens called Maquis to sabotage the German occupation. Audie Murphy, an American soldier, described his unit's advance across France: "Smarting under the wrongs and indignities endured during the years of German occupation, members of the French underground now emerge from their hiding and strike. Sometimes we find whole towns liberated . . . and waiting for our entrance. Maquis join our forces as guides and give us information on enemy strongholds."

But the closer the Allied Army came to Germany, the more fiercely the German troops fought. The fight beyond France's borders would become even bloodier.

Did You Know . . .

- Operation Torch marked the first time that military commanders from the United States and the United Kingdom coordinated an invasion together. The operation also involved the first large-scale use of United States paratroopers when the 509th Parachute Regiment dropped onto the airfields outside Oran, Algeria.

- Audie Murphy of Texas remains the most decorated soldier in US history. He fought in North Africa, Italy, France, and Belgium, earning 28 medals including the Congressional Medal of Honor, all before turning 21 years old. After WWII, the famous veteran starred in 44 Hollywood movies and wrote a bestseller about his combat experiences called *To Hell and Back*.

- The oldest man to land in Normandy during the first wave of the D-Day attack was 56 years old. He was Gen. Teddy Roosevelt, Jr, the only general to land in the first wave. The son of former US President Teddy Roosevelt, he received a Medal of Honor for his actions on D-Day.

- To prevent an Allied landing in Western Europe, Hitler ordered the construction of the Atlantic Wall. The Wall stretched from France to Norway, but France received extra fortifications as Allied troops would need to organize nearby in the United Kingdom. The Wall in France included thick concrete bunkers containing artillery protected by over six million landmines.

- Sergeant J. D. Salinger rode in the second wave of landings on D-Day. He carried inside his shirt the first several chapters of a novel he was writing entitled *The Catcher in the Rye*. Published in 1951, the novel has remained popular and is often assigned in high school literature classes.
- Lt. James Doohan landed on D-Day with the 3rd Canadian Infantry Division. The enemy fire cut off the middle finger on Doohan's right hand. After the war, Doohan became an actor. Most famously, he played Chief Engineer Montgomery Scott (aka "Scotty") on the television show *Star Trek* in the 1960s. Clever camera work hid the hand with the missing finger.

BATTLE OF THE BULGE

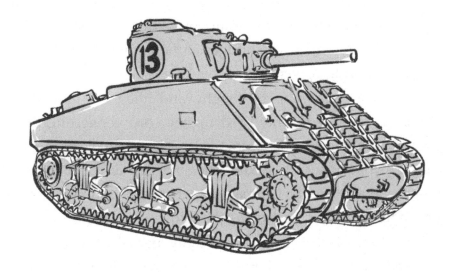

As the American and British armies, joined by the Free French and other Allies, rolled through France, Gen. Eisenhower and Gen. Montgomery debated their next move.

Eisenhower and his officers believed a direct strike toward Germany made the most sense. For the Americans, a straight road to Berlin would bring the quickest victory. But Montgomery and his officers wanted to liberate Holland before turning into Germany. For the British, clearing the German military from areas along the English Channel ensured the safety of the United Kingdom.

To ease the worries of the United Kingdom, Gen. Eisenhower agreed to Gen. Montgomery's plan. The British commander would spearhead an offensive into Holland. Montgomery called the plan Operation Market Garden.

The plan was very ambitious. Launched in September 1944, the attack called for a massive wave of paratroopers to capture bridges along a 62-mile road deep into enemy territory. These drops occurred at Eindhoven, 13 miles from the front, at Nijmegen, 53 miles from the front, and Arnhem, about 60 miles at the end of the road. The bridges at these towns, along with a few smaller bridges, were key to the Allies' success.

While the paratroopers fought and died to take these crossings, an Allied Army sped up the road connecting these towns. Speed and surprise were the keys to the whole campaign. The army needed to secure the bridges and relieve the paratroopers before the German military responded by trapping the paratroopers and destroying the bridges.

Operation Market Garden was only partially successful. It liberated parts of Holland. But the Allies failed to grab the final bridgehead needed to advance into Germany. The road into Holland was bordered by muddy areas that prevented tanks from going far into the countryside. This allowed the German military to slow the advance of the main army by concentrating on the Allied column and blocking its way.

With the Allies stalled Hitler looked for ways to push them away. The Nazi leader had grown desperate. The Red Army was preparing to cross into Germany from the east. The Americans and British were on the verge of entering Germany from the west.

Hitler gambled that he could draw troops from the Eastern Front and throw them at the Allies gathered in Belgium's

Ardennes Forest. With some luck, he thought the German military could press the American and British armies against the English Channel and quickly destroy a chunk of these forces before returning the German soldiers to the Eastern Front.

For this to work, he needed to strike during a stretch of bad winter weather. The Allies had achieved air supremacy by knocking out the Luftwaffe. The German military could only have a chance for success if the Allied planes could not fly. The awful conditions of December 1944 were perfect for the German ground assault. About eight inches of snow sat on the ground in temperatures near 20 F.

The American Army bore the brunt of the German assault. The initial attack wave included 410,000 soldiers equipped with 1,400 tanks, assault guns, and tank destroyers. The German Army also had 2,600 artillery pieces and 1,600 anti-tank guns for added firepower.

Not expecting an offensive, especially in awful winter weather, the US Army of 610,000 troops was caught off guard by Hitler's aggressive move. The German panzers, or tanks, pierced the American frontlines. Crack troops of the Waffen-SS, elite units of armed fanatics devoted to the Nazi Party, plowed through the heavy snow, laying siege to pockets of the US Army that resisted the onslaught. The offensive captured at least 23,000 US soldiers.

The Nazi Army managed to put a bulge in the Allied line 50 miles wide and 70 miles deep, giving the battle its name.

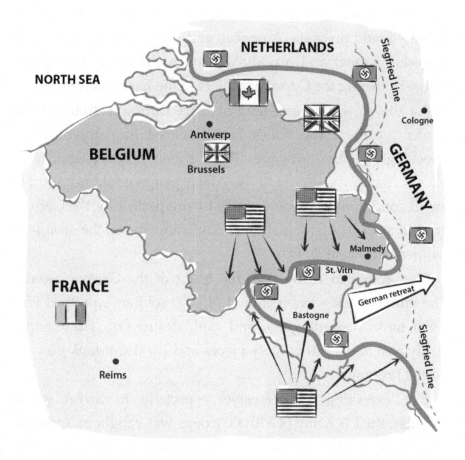

The incredible success of the offensive met one major snag at a crossroads town called Bastogne, Belgium. The 101st Airborne commanded by US Gen. Anthony McAuliffe, along with several other units, defended the town. Troops in Bastogne stubbornly resisted despite heavy shelling. For a week, Bastogne sat under siege. A German general sent a request for Gen. McAuliffe to surrender the roughly 20,000 Americans in the town or face even heavier attacks. McAuliffe responded with one word: "NUTS!"

The besieged Americans in Bastogne clogged the roadways needed by the German Army to transport supplies to their frontline units beyond the town. The holdouts in the Belgian town boosted the morale of US troops throughout the army.

To rescue Gen. McAuliffe's men, Gen. Eisenhower ordered Gen. George S. Patton to break the siege. Patton was the US Army's best tank commander. He had successfully campaigned in North Africa and Sicily. Patton's 3rd Army spearheaded a rapid drive across France after landing in Normandy. Now near the German border, Patton pivoted his tanks and drove them hard toward Bastogne. His tanks broke the siege.

Although the German commanders had successfully gathered their forces without alerting the British and American armies at the start of the offensive, the Nazis had few reserves to throw into the assault as combat wore down the units. They also had a few extra units to add pressure on any Allied holdouts like those in Bastogne or to block a counterattack like that from Gen. Patton's troops. One German general later explained, "There were no adequate reinforcements, no supplies of ammunition, and although the number of armored divisions was high, their strength in tanks was low - it was largely paper strength."

The heavy losses taken by the German Army as they hit the Allies' defensive positions were unsustainable. About 98,000 German soldiers had become casualties, roughly a quarter of the initial attack force. Nazi Germany simply did not have the manpower to replace these troops. The attack through the Ardennes Forest was the last offensive launched by the German military during WWII.

As the Nazi Army lost momentum, the Americans contained and then closed the bulge in their lines. But the cost in lives was staggering. The US suffered 89,000 casualties. Of these, over 19,000 were killed.

The month-long Battle of the Bulge was the most intense fighting faced by the American military in Europe. And the US had won. Now the focus was on ending the war by crossing the Rhine River and pushing deep into the heartland of Nazi Germany.

Did You Know . . .

- The M4 Sherman tank was the most widely used tank in the US Army during WWII. Over 50,000 Shermans were built between 1942 and 1945. Through the Lend-Lease Act, Shermans appeared in the militaries of the United Kingdom, Free France, China, and the Soviet Union. The tank was named after US Gen. William Tecumseh Sherman of the American Civil War.

- Dangerously low on gasoline and vehicles, the German military used roughly 50,000 horses to power their supply lines during the Battle of the Bulge. Horses had the added benefit of being able to move more quickly through the thick woods and heavy snow. The available gasoline was reserved for use by the German tank units.

- To surprise the American Army and quickly overrun their defenses, the Germans used a few dozen English-speaking commandos dressed in captured American uniforms. They drove captured US jeeps. These commandoes sped through the Americans spreading misinformation and sabotaging equipment.

- Under intense pressure to halt the German offensive, Gen. Dwight Eisenhower authorized the use of African American troops to replace casualties suffered by US units during the Battle of the Bulge. Over 2,000 African Americans volunteered. For the first time in modern US military history, African Americans and Whites served as equals in the same units.

- The Waffen-SS units of Nazi fanatics committed several war crimes during the Battle of the Bulge. Most infamously, these Germans killed 84 American prisoners on December 17, 1944, near Malmedy, Belgium. This became known as the Malmedy Massacre. US units retaliated. Near Chenogne, Belgium, American soldiers allegedly killed around 60 German prisoners on January 1, 1945.
- After WWII, Gen. Dwight Eisenhower ran for US President, serving two terms from 1953 until 1961. One of his greatest accomplishments as President was the creation of the Interstate Highway System to facilitate trade and rapid troop movements in case of an invasion. Eisenhower promoted the system after seeing the highways, or autobahns, built in Germany during the 1930s.

THE HOLOCAUST

By 1945, the Soviet Union had closed in on Berlin along the Eastern Front. The Americans and British, along with the other Allied nations, pushed into Germany along the Western Front. Both soon discovered the horrors of the Holocaust and the so-called Final Solution enacted by believers in racist Nazi ideas.

Nazi Germany had carried out a program of extermination of Jewish people and others considered genetically inferior. Hitler and his henchmen believed that the future of Germany required eliminating from the gene pool anyone seen as defective or weaker. Nazi scientists considered these inferior peoples to be like a virus infecting the German nation. Removal and extermination would allow supposedly pure-blooded Germans to prosper.

The Nazis believed, according to the perverted science backed by Hitler, that the Aryans represented the master race, possessing supposedly superior intelligence and health. The Aryans were defined as people of northern European origin typically having blond hair and blue eyes. Of course, the Nazis argued that Germans were predominantly Aryan. The Nazis wanted to purge the country of any non-Aryans who, through intermarriage, were believed to dilute and corrupt the German bloodline.

Some of the earliest targets of Hitler's racist ideas were children of African descent born of French colonial troops and German women. France had stationed these colonial troops in western Germany along an occupied area known as the Rhineland. For several years at the end of WWI, France guarded this area to prevent another German invasion.

In 1935, the Nazis passed the Nuremberg Laws forbidding Germans from marrying Jews and declaring that only Germans could be citizens. Anyone with ancestry traced to Jews, Africans, or Romani, an ethnic group in eastern Europe, was specifically targeted. This gave a legal justification for Nazi racism.

After the reign of terror on Kristallnacht in 1938, Hitler organized a systematic campaign of rounding up all those considered racially inferior. Jews were the primary target, serving as scapegoats for everything the Nazis claimed was wrong with Germany.

To separate the millions of Jews from the supposedly pure German race, Hitler authorized ghettos in the major cities. To

114

leave Germany, Jewish families and individuals had to surrender half or more of their wealth. But even if they could afford to travel abroad to start over their lives, no foreign country was willing to accept so many millions of refugees.

Forced to move into ghettos, Jewish families had to leave most of their property and belongings behind. This property was confiscated by the Nazis. Loyal members of the Nazi party either purchased or received for free their homes, furniture, and other goods. Any profits from sales went to the government, not to the Jewish owners.

Life in the ghetto was harsh. Families lived in crowded conditions. The Nazis allowed them few supplies. All Jews were forced to wear an arm badge with yellow triangles that mimicked the Star of David, a symbol prominent within Jewish culture. This allowed Nazi guards and the public to easily identify them.

Other groups targeted by the Nazis also had to wear armbands. Persons identified as gay were required to wear a pink triangle. Criminals wore green triangles. Romani had brown triangles. Jehovah's Witnesses had purple triangles. Political prisoners wore red triangles since the Nazis most often targeted communists, and red was the color of their movement.

As Germany invaded Poland and other countries, the Nazis encountered local Jewish populations that they wanted to be removed. Hitler looked for what he called "lebensraum," translated as "living space," for the German people. The pursuit of "lebensraum" justified his invasions. This was especially true for eastern parts of Europe populated, according to the Nazi view, by a large number of racially inferior peoples.

Einsatzgruppen, meaning task forces, followed behind the advancing German Army when they invaded Poland in 1939. Einsatzgruppen served under the authority of the SS and worked as an execution squad, putting into action the racist ideology of the Nazi Party. From September through December 1939, the task forces rolling through Poland murdered around 50,000 Poles, including 7,000 Jews living in Poland.

In September 1941, as Operation Barbarossa sent the German war machine advancing into the Soviet Union, Hitler authorized the railroads to transport Jews from Germany, Austria, and Czechoslovakia to German-occupied Poland and the Soviet Union. Hitler believed he was purifying these areas as part of his effort to build an enlarged Germany. The SS and Gestapo, the German secret police, also arranged with the military to execute civilians deemed racially inferior in occupied areas.

Again, the Einsatzgruppen went to work as German troops pushed further into eastern Europe. They executed communist officials as well as Jews, whether they were old men, women, or babies. Estimates show that these death squads killed around 1.5 million Jews in the Nazi-occupied Soviet Union.

The Nazis did not question the inhumanity of this murder. Instead, they pondered faster ways of killing. By 1941, Nazi leaders observed post-traumatic stress in personnel who did executions by firing squad. Also, the German military expressed concerns about the waste of ammunition in a war in which metals and gunpowder were resources not easily replaced. The Nazi regime experimented with special trucks that used exhaust fumes to suffocate people crowded into the rear compartment.

But this also placed the Einsatzgruppen too close to the murdering, causing them distress over their killing spree.

In March 1933, the first concentration camp, Dachau, opened outside of Munich, Germany. It was used primarily for political prisoners and was the longest-running camp in operation, until its liberation in April 1945.

How to accomplish the elimination of millions of human beings was settled at a meeting at a villa outside of Berlin on January 20, 1942. The Wannsee Conference gathered 15 high-ranking Nazi Party members and government officials to sort out the logistics of extermination. The Conference informed officials and gained their support for what was called the "Final Solution" to the problem of supposedly racially inferior peoples present in Europe. At the time of the Wannsee Conference, most participants were already aware that the Nazi regime had engaged in the mass murder of Jews and other civilians in the German-occupied areas of the Soviet Union and Serbia. Some had learned of the actions of the *Einsatzgruppen* and other police and military units, which were already slaughtering tens of thousands of Jews in the German-occupied Soviet Union. Others were aware that units of the German Army and the SS and the police were killing Jews in Serbia. None of the officials present at the meeting objected to the "Final Solution" that Heydrich announced.

The racially undesirable and political opponents of the Nazi regime would be herded from ghettos into concentration camps and execution camps.

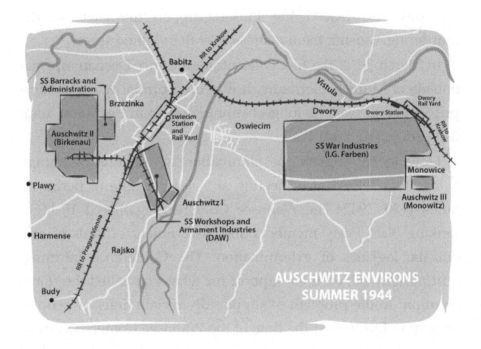

Labeled on map: Babitz, RR to Krakow, SS Barracks and Administration, Brzezinka, Vistula, Dwory Rail Yard, Oswiecim Station and Rail Yard, Dwory, Dwory Station, RR to Krakow, Auschwitz II (Birkenau), Oswiecim, SS War Industries (I.G. Farben), Plawy, Monowice, Auschwitz III (Monowitz), Auschwitz I, SS Workshops and Armament Industries (DAW), Harmense, RR to Prague-Vienna, Rajsko, AUSCHWITZ ENVIRONS SUMMER 1944, Budy

The Nazis established three killing stations in occupied Poland located at Belzec, Sobibor, and Treblinka. All along the eastern areas captured by Nazi Germany, people were crowded into railroad cars and shipped to the death camps. Arrivals were separated by sex. Men went in one direction. Women and children went in another direction. The parting of families at gunpoint with guard dogs snapping at the arrivals made for a living horror. Goods carried or worn by the largely Jewish captives were confiscated.

The people taken to the camps deemed unfit to work were then crowded naked into large shower rooms. But instead of receiving water, poisonous gas was pumped into the rooms. The system allowed for killing large numbers of people without alerting them to their imminent doom. Some 1.5 million Jews died at Belzec, Sobibor, and Treblinka. The Nazis instructed doctors to remove any gold fillings from the teeth of the dead. Money collected from these gold fillings helped fund the German war effort.

To clear the gas chambers, the camp organizers regularly used Jews considered healthy and strong to undertake the ordeal of cleaning the gas chambers for a new batch of victims. The Jews selected were forced to keep the flow of people through the extermination camps going steadily.

Also, though the camp commander might be German, many of the guards or officers overseeing camp operations were non-Germans. Rather than expose Germans to the trauma of operating the camps, Nazi officials often used local Nazi sympathizers from occupied areas. This kept many in the German public from fully realizing the horrors of the extermination campaign waged by Hitler and his henchmen.

In many parts of eastern Europe, the Nazis were seen as liberators, not invaders. Areas like Ukraine, Lithuania, Latvia, Estonia, and eastern Poland, among other parts of eastern Europe, had been under the control of the Soviet Union. Some, like Lithuania, Latvia, and Estonia, had won independence after WWI. In the nonaggression deal with Hitler in 1939, Stalin won Hitler's support for taking the eastern part of Poland. In June 1940, with France and most of western Europe conquered by the German blitzkrieg, Stalin's Red Army invaded Lithuania, Latvia, and Estonia. When Hitler launched Operation Barbarossa in 1941, many in these Soviet occupied-areas embraced the Nazis.

Now, as German troops rolled deep into the Soviet Union, Nazi sympathizers aided the Germans by hunting Jews and other so-called undesirables. These collaborators helped run the death camps.

Jews and others sent to the various concentration camps operated by the Nazis shared a terrifying experience.

Holocaust survivor Eva Mozes Kor confronted the horrors of Auschwitz, outside Krakow, Poland. Auschwitz emerged as the most notorious death camp, where up to 6,000 people a day were killed in gas chambers. Those inmates considered strong enough were spared execution. Instead, these individuals joined forced labor squads providing supplies to the German war effort.

Kor made it out of Auschwitz at the end of WWII because she and her sister were identical twins. Nazi doctors were fascinated by identical twins. They conducted painful and dangerous experiments on such twins for their genetic tests. Kor survived knowing that each day might be her last because "nobody made any secret of the fact that we would be terminated when we were no longer useful." She endured frequent medical experiments, regularly receiving injections with unknown substances. To Nazi scientists, she was like a lab rat. Her life had little value.

During her time inside Auschwitz, Kor was surrounded by death. She later wrote, "My first initiation to death had come when the SS had their dog kill the lady who fell out of line. Since then, I had seen the bodies of the children who had died in the barracks, the many bodies wheeled by each day on the death carts, and I had even seen the bodies of prisoners who had thrown themselves on the electrified fencing to escape Auschwitz."

As Nazi Germany sent more and more of its able-bodied men to die at the front, workers were in shorter and shorter supply. Concentration camps served as forced labor camps with inmates literally worked to death. Some Jews and others held by the Nazis were sent outside the camps to work at factories producing essential goods for the war, like ammunition or clothes.

Survivor Gerda Weissman Klein of Poland recalled being herded onto a train on her way to a factory in eastern Germany after the Nazi's invasion. Upon reaching her destination, the enslaved Jewish laborers were marched through a small town to their future workplaces. Klein recalled the townspeople's reaction: "People looked at us as though they had not expected us to be human. Children were called into houses." A woman watering her plants froze, staring with wide eyes. Klein never forgot this woman: "Brought up under the Nazis, she expected us to be monsters. What a shock it must have been to find us looking very much like herself, some of us quite pretty."

As the US Army rolled into Germany, the horrors of the Holocaust became undeniable. A medical officer who helped liberate the Dachau concentration camp in southern Germany stood stunned: "A row of small cement structures near the prison entrance contained a coal-fired crematorium, a gas chamber disguised as a shower, and a room piled high with naked and emaciated human corpses." Everywhere he looked, he saw horror. He reported, "As I turned to look over the prison yard with unbelieving eyes, I saw a large number of dead inmates lying where they had fallen in the last few hours or days before our arrival. Since all the many bodies were in various stages of decomposition, the stench of death was overpowering."

Survivor Gerda Weissman Klein cherished the memory of her liberation from the Nazis. One day in 1945, the German officers and soldiers suddenly vanished.

The Americans were approaching. A US officer arrived at the gates of the factory where she worked.

Within an hour, Red Cross ambulances arrived. Klein, weighing only 68 pounds at the time of liberation, remembered the scene: "In a trance, I walked to a truck and got in. On the soldiers' sleeves was a red diamond, the insignia of the Fifth U.S. Infantry Division. Their uniforms, their language, their kindness and concern made it true: we were finally free!"

In total, the Nazi regime murdered over six million people of Jewish ancestry, nearly 70% of the Jewish population in Europe and a third of all Jews in the world.

Gen. Eisenhower and other American generals agreed that it was extremely important to document the Holocaust. Teams of photographers arrived at the death camps to preserve evidence of the war crimes committed by the Nazi regime.

Films documented the atrocities as well. American units forced German residents from nearby towns to walk through the camps. This ensured they could never deny the systemic murder of millions by Hitler and his supporters.

To bring the Nazis responsible for the mass killing to justice, the Allies organized the Nuremberg Trials. Nuremberg, Germany, had played a prominent role in the rise of the Nazis. Several famous rallies were held in the city during the 1930s. The most infamous gathering occurred in 1934, early in Hitler's leadership of Germany.

This rally emphasized Germany's unity with the Nazi party, introduced the Nazi leadership to the world, and broadcast Hitler's style and views to the global community via a ground-breaking propaganda film called *Triumph of the Will*.

From 1945 through 1946, an international military tribunal organized by the United States, France, the United Kingdom, and the Soviet Union tried 21 of the most prominent Nazis.

The court documented the charges of international aggression and the evils that resulted from the Nazi war effort. The defendants also faced multiple charges of war crimes. US Supreme Court Justice Robert H. Jackson acted as chief prosecutor.

Of the 21 defendants, 19 were convicted. Of these, 12 received the death sentence while three received life terms in prison. The rest received prison sentences ranging from 10 to 20 years. The inmates were incarcerated at Spandau Prison in Berlin.

From 1946 until 1949, the United States conducted 12 additional military trials at Nuremberg. These included 177 high-ranking Nazis, including doctors, judges, businessmen, bureaucrats, and military officers. These trials focused largely on the role of the defendants in carrying out the Holocaust.

Did You Know . . .

- Gerda Weismann Klein married a Jewish man who fled Germany before WWII. He served as an officer in the 5th US Infantry Division, helping to liberate the enslaved labor camp where Klein lived. They married and moved to Buffalo, New York. In 1957, Klein published her memoir *All But My Life* about her ordeal under the Nazis.

- Holocaust survivor Simon Wiesenthal dedicated his life after the war to hunting Nazi officials responsible for the Holocaust and bringing them to justice. He and other Nazi hunters tracked the commanders and guards from the camps, who often changed their names at the end of WWII and blended into society, including moving to the United States.

- The public display of the swastika, the symbol of the Nazi Party, has been banned in Germany since WWII. The symbol can be used inside Buddhist and Hindu religious temples since its ancient meaning in eastern societies of Asia refers to good luck and wellness.

- After WWII, the Allies worked to establish Israel in the Middle East as a predominantly Jewish refuge that could give voice to the global Jewish population. Israel was carved from the colony of Palestine, which had a large Muslim population, claimed by the United Kingdom. This has led to decades of conflict between the Jewish and Muslim communities.

- The Steven Spielberg film *Schindler's List* from 1993 tells the true story of Oskar Schindler, a Nazi supporter, who used the forced labor of Jews in his enamelware and ammunition factories. Schindler became horrified by the Holocaust and began using the jobs to protect Jews from death. He is credited with saving around 1,200 lives.

- The largest population of Jewish people outside of Israel lives in the United States. To document the Holocaust as survivors aged, the United States Holocaust Memorial Museum opened in Washington, D. C., in April 1993. The Museum aims to teach younger generations about the horrors of genocide in order to promote respect for life and human dignity.

BERLIN

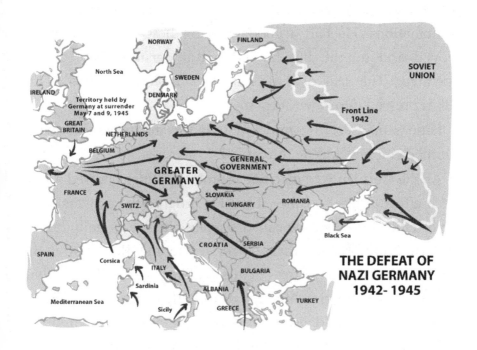

German Gen. Hasso von Manteuffel, who worked closely with Hitler and spearheaded the failed offensive during the Battle of the Bulge, explained the Nazi leader's strengths as a military commander: "Hitler had read a lot of military literature, and was also fond of listening to military lectures. In this way, coupled with his personal experience of the last war [WWI] as an ordinary soldier, he gained a very good knowledge of the lower level of warfare - the properties of different weapons; the effect of ground and weather; the mentality and morale of troops."

Such skills allowed Hitler's Nazi Germany to conquer much of Europe in the early years of WWII.

But Hitler's major flaw was his inability to wage a war over a prolonged period. This made him blind and reckless about Germany's supply of people and resources. Manteuffel stressed that Hitler "had no idea of the higher strategical and tactical combinations. He had a good grasp of how a single division moved and fought, but he did not understand how armies operated." That lack of skill became increasingly evident as the Allies pressed into Nazi Germany.

Hitler's many shortcomings now led to the leveling of major German cities, including the capital.

As the German war machine crumbled, Hitler ordered a last-ditch effort to hold off the Allies. He ordered the conversion of major cities into what he called fortress cities, especially on the Eastern Front. Rather than surrender to the Red Army, the soldiers in these fortress cities, along with the civilian populations, were to fight to the death rather than surrender. He hoped this would delay the advance of the Soviet Union to Berlin. He also believed the United States and the United Kingdom might join with Nazi Germany in a war against the advancing Soviet Union given the distrust between capitalists and communists.

But Hitler's plan to fortify the major cities failed to slow the Soviet juggernaut. Stalin and his commanders refused to take the bait by wasting men and resources slugging it out with the German military in unnecessary urban combat. Instead, the Soviets encircled the cities and hammered them with artillery, proceeding slowly into the downtown areas. Meanwhile, the

Red Army remained focused on reaching Berlin as soon as possible. The faster Berlin fell and Hitler was killed or captured, the sooner the war in Europe would end.

To accomplish Germany's massive resistance, Hitler directed boys and girls as young as 12 years old to defend the barricaded streets. The German military simply did not have any more bodies to pull into the ranks other than young kids and the elderly. But while the elderly now looked with doubt at Hitler's disastrous wars, the young more often accepted the call to action with enthusiasm.

An organization known as the Hitler Youth had long taught Germany's children about Nazi ideas and trained them in basic military tactics. The propaganda taught to these thousands of young, impressionable Germans for the last decade now led them into the slaughter of modern warfare. Hitler ordered kids to defend the country even though they lacked adequate equipment, training, or leadership. The Red Army showed them no mercy.

A Berlin resident observed the Hitler Youth in action in April 1945. The kids "patrol the streets in groups of six with rifles over their shoulders. No adults are watching over them, so they do whatever they want," he continued, "the young children go around wearing heavy steel soldier's helmets on their heads. It's a heartbreaking sight."

Many of these children would be killed along with the last remnants of the Wehrmacht and SS units. The Red Army steadily advanced block-by-block through Berlin toward Hitler's command bunker. One witness marveled at the raging street battle: "The air is heavy with smoke. Everywhere around us is the crackle of small arms fire. Russian artillery is pouring an almost constant barrage into the heart of the city." The dead littered the city.

As the Soviet troops rolled into Berlin and other parts of eastern Germany, thousands of Germans fled, if they could manage, to the Americans and British in the western part of Germany. The years of vicious warfare between Nazi Germany and the Soviet Union had turned the fighting in the east into a war of vengeance.

The racist policies of the Nazis that had caused them to destroy Russian villages and abuse, even murder, inhabitants when they invaded gave the Red Army little reason to be anything but brutal within the now-conquered German territories. Soviet soldiers retaliated by subjecting German civilians to beatings, murder, and various other cruelties. As one person observed late in the war, Germans "fear the Russians as no nation has ever feared a conquering army."

As the Soviets hammered the Germans defending Berlin, the Western Allies started 1945 by seeking a firm bridgehead across the Rhine River. The wide, fast-flowing river formed a strong natural barrier that the Nazi military could easily defend. But when word came of a major bridge at Remagen, Germany, that remained intact, the US Army rushed to capture it. Through some luck and faulty wiring of explosives installed by German military engineers, an attempt to destroy the bridge as the Americans approached did not succeed.

With the bridge at Remagen taken, the Western Allies led by the Americans poured into Germany. Tank columns rolled rapidly through the countryside. German armies in the area had been exhausted by the Battle of the Bulge. No reinforcements existed to restore their ability to hold off the US and UK troops. Much of the remaining Nazi Army now fought a life-or-death struggle to hold Berlin.

Hitler knew that his time as leader of Germany was over. From his bunker, he could hear and feel the rumble of artillery closing in on his position. Hitler could not bear to see a future without Nazism. He took his own life on April 30, 1945, rather than be captured. German troops burned Hitler's corpse to prevent the Red Army from displaying the dead Fuhrer of Germany.

The Nazi regime fought on for another week. On May 8, 1945, Nazi Germany unconditionally surrendered to the Allies. V-E Day, short for Victory in Europe, had finally come.

But WWII was not yet over.

Did You Know . . .

- The T-34 tank produced by the Soviet Union is widely recognized as one of WWII's best tanks. It was also the most produced tank of WWII, with the Soviets making nearly 60,000 by the end of the war. In the 1990s, 27 countries still used T-34s, demonstrating the effectiveness of the model.
- The most common rifle used by the US during WWII was the M1 Garland. It became a standard issue by the US Army in 1936. The weapon was the first semiautomatic rifle adopted by the US military. More than 5.4 million M1 Garlands, each weighing 9.5 pounds, were manufactured until 1957 when it was replaced as the standard issue.
- The industrial heartland of Germany is in the Ruhr Valley in the western part of the country. Once the United States crossed the Rhine River at Remagen, the nearby Ruhr factories and mineral resources such as coal quickly fell to the Allies, stripping the Nazi war machine of much of its ability to resupply.
- After Hitler died, Admiral Karl Donitz, supreme commander of the German navy, took control of the Nazi government and military. He surrendered on May 7, 1945, but stayed in charge until May 23 to encourage the surrender of all German units. He was sentenced to 10 years at the Nuremberg Trials for allowing enslaved labor at German shipyards.
- The battle for Castle Itter is considered the strangest clash of WWII. The Austrian castle served as a small prison, mainly holding French citizens including Charles DeGaulle's sister.

The US Army liberated the prison. When the Waffen-SS attacked, liberated prisoners and surrendered Wehrmacht troops joined the Americans in defending the castle.

- To prevent Austria's famous Lipizzaner horses from falling to the Red Army, the US Army launched Operation Cowboy in April 1945. The operation was a raid 20 miles deep into Nazi-held territory to capture the herd. Wehrmacht troops quickly surrendered at the farm and joined the American troops in fighting Waffen-SS soldiers who tried to recapture the horses.

OKINAWA

To prepare for an expected invasion of mainland Japan, the US military eyed the large island of Okinawa roughly 400 miles south of the country. Okinawa was needed as a staging area to gather supplies and soldiers for the massive invasion to come. The island also gave the US Navy a base from which to cut supply routes between mainland Japan and the Japanese military fighting in China and Korea.

The initial invasion of Okinawa on April 1, 1945, was the biggest amphibious landing in the Pacific Theater during WWII. The US Marines and army troops faced little opposition on the beaches. Instead, the Imperial Japanese forces had prepared heavy defensive strongholds away from the shores where the US naval battleships and other warships could not effectively bombard the positions.

The battle quickly earned a nickname - "typhoon of steel" - for the intensity of the fighting both on land and on sea. Some 70,000 Imperial Japanese soldiers positioned in caves and other defensive positions hammered the 250,000 American troops sent ashore during the fighting.

Just as Hitler had activated the Hitler Youth as part of his last-ditch effort to hold off the Allies, the Imperial Japanese commanders mobilized around 2,000 teenagers for frontline service. Boys joined the Blood and Iron Imperial Corps. These teens transported supplies, repaired communication cables, and delivered messages, among other tasks. Girls served in the Lily Corps, becoming nurses. Roughly half of the kids used by the Imperial Japanese military died in the fighting.

In an attempt to trap the US troops marching across the island, the Imperial Japanese launched waves of kamikazes against the Allied fleet, numbering over 1,600 ships. The intense ground combat forced the Allied ships to sit offshore in support of the troops. Part of the Imperial Japanese strategy at Okinawa was to inflict as much damage on the fleet as possible in order to degrade its effectiveness for any future landings against mainland Japan.

Kamikazes, meaning "divine wind" in Japanese, were combat aircraft on a suicide mission. The pilot guided the plane loaded with fuel and explosives toward vital parts of a ship for maximum damage. Such attacks were the desperate last option as Imperial Japan could not afford to replace the planes or pilots.

Waves of kamikazes terrorized Allied sailors. Over 1,500 kamikazes rained down on the warships. At Okinawa, the US Navy suffered the heaviest losses ever from a single battle with almost 5,000 sailors killed. 149 Allied ships were either hit or sunk by the crashing planes, with the several dozen ships destroyed being smaller vessels.

The Japanese had built a number of defensive lines across the island with deep underground tunnels and artillery positioned in caves, making these units hard to destroy. The most important fortification centered on Shuri Castle, the headquarters for the Japanese commanders on the island.

The 500-year-old castle had been the seat of the royal court governing Okinawa and carried huge significance for island residents and the Imperial Japanese forces.

Combat raged for 82 days with Okinawa finally secured by the US military on June 22, 1945. The Americans needed to stage costly ground assaults to clear the Japanese lines.

During the battle, Americans sustained more than 49,000 casualties, with over 12,500 killed or missing. Of the Imperial Japanese forces defending the island, around 110,000 died, again preferring death to the dishonor of surrender.

Civilian casualties were equally staggering. Nearly 150,000 Okinawans died in the fighting, about half of the island's total population. Often, Imperial Japanese forces used civilians as human shields. Japanese propaganda also spread fear about the advancing Americans.

The Japanese described Americans as violent, racist conquerors who would torture captives. Many terrified Okinawans committed suicide as US units approached. Some mothers even jumped off cliffs while they clutched their children. The scenes traumatized the Americans who tried to convince these civilians that they would not be harmed.

As the Allied military regrouped after the heavy fighting in the thick mud of Okinawa, commanders and political leaders turned to the question of launching the final island hop of the

Pacific campaign - an assault on mainland Japan that would end
WWII.

Did You Know . . .

- Calvin Graham, born in Canton, Texas, on April 3, 1930, was the youngest person to enlist in the US military during WWII. He lied about his age and joined the US Navy at 12 years old in 1942. He served on the battleship *USS South Dakota* and was wounded in the naval battle off Guadalcanal before being discovered and discharged.

- Many of the US marines and US army troops fighting on Okinawa were from the southern parts of the United States. When they captured Shuri Castle, the main defensive line of the Imperial Japanese forces, the Americans first raised the Confederate battle flag over the position before US commanders quickly replaced it with the US flag.

- The most common aircraft in the Japanese air forces was the Mitsubishi A6M Zero, the first carrier-based combat plane that could outmaneuver land-based planes. The Allies did not develop a fighter plane to counter the Zero until 1943. Japan built 10,430 Zeroes, the preferred plane for kamikaze attacks.

- The last Japanese soldier to surrender was Hiroo Onoda, an intelligence officer serving in the Philippines. He, along with three other soldiers, refused to believe that Japan had surrendered. They hid deep in the jungle and conducted guerilla attacks for the next 30 years. Only after Onoda's former commanding officer flew to the Philippines did Onoda surrender - in 1974.

- The invasion by Imperial Japan of the Dutch East Indies, now Indonesia, cut off the Allies from a major region of rubber production. The US government responded by investing $700 million in 51 plants producing synthetic rubber from petroleum byproducts. Synthetic rubber proved vital to the war effort. For instance, a WWII tank required 2,000 pounds of rubber.
- Vesta Stoudt, a mom with sons in the US Navy, worked at an ordnance plant in Illinois when she noticed that the tape used on ammunition boxes easily tore when wet. To fix this problem, she invented duct tape, named for being waterproof. Duct tape became a quick-fix solution to damaged items during WWII.

THE MANHATTAN PROJECT

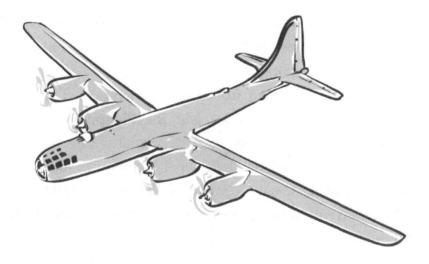

Paul Tibbets described the experience of a bomber pilot and crew as they rained explosives down on enemy cities: "To the men who fly the bombers, targets are inanimate, consisting of buildings, bridges, docks, factories, railroad yards." People from several miles above were largely "invisible." But the bombing raid over Hiroshima, Japan, set for August 6, 1945, was very different.

President Harry Truman, who assumed office after President Roosevelt died from a cerebral hemorrhage on April 12, 1945, okayed Tibbets's mission after debating the risks of a mainland invasion. As Roosevelt's Vice-President now sitting in the US's highest political office, Truman lacked the clout of Roosevelt, who had been in the White House for over 12 years. Truman did not want to appear weak or indecisive. Truman also understood that Americans were tired of war. Worse, the endgame for any conflict usually is the bloodiest time in an armed struggle.

Military advisors painted a bleak picture for Truman. Calling the invasion of Japan Operation Downfall, strategists warned Truman "that operations in this area will be opposed not only by the available organized military forces of the Empire but also by a fanatically hostile population."

Using estimates drawn from the experience of fighting the Imperial Japanese at Okinawa and the Philippines, advisors informed Truman to expect a 35% casualty rate. Defeating mainland Japan would risk between 1.7 million to four million American casualties, with a range of 400,000 to 800,00 combat deaths. Japan would suffer between five and 10 million killed.

So horrific were the estimates, some planners called for strangling Imperial Japan with a naval blockade and air raids before launching an invasion. In their view, an assault on mainland Japan should only occur in 1947 or 1948 to minimize casualties. But military commanders and political leaders believed prolonging the war would hurt American morale and that of the Allies, already strained by four years of death and sacrifice.

Worse, for Truman, President Roosevelt had negotiated a deal with Stalin at the Yalta Conference in February 1945 that called for the Soviet Union to attack Imperial Japan six months after the surrender of Nazi Germany. Just as the US landings at Normandy eased pressure on the Red Army along the Eastern Front by opening up the Western Front, Roosevelt hoped a

Soviet invasion of northern Japan would ease resistance against the US assault in southern Japan.

Truman now faced the reality that a prolonged attack on Japan would involve the Soviet Union joining the war in the Pacific. This would likely lead to a divided Japan similar to the hardening divide between capitalist Allies in western-occupied Germany and the communist Soviet Union in eastern-occupied Germany.

This divide too grew out of the Yalta Conference. Roosevelt and Churchill had agreed to Stalin's position that the Soviet Union should have influence over eastern European countries conquered by the Red Army in return for the Soviet Union's assistance in the war against Japan.

This agreement was confirmed at the Potsdam Conference held outside Berlin in Summer 1945. This meeting of Truman, Churchill, and Stalin arranged to divide Germany into four zones: three western zones each controlled by the UK, France, and US as well as one eastern zone controlled by the Soviet Union. Berlin, as Germany's capital, was also divided into four zones of control operated by these major Allies. Countries such as Poland, Romania, Hungary, Bulgaria, and Czechoslovakia fell under Soviet control as Stalin wanted a buffer zone to ensure that a postwar Germany could never strike deep into Russia again.

Finally, Truman had recently learned of the Manhattan Project.

German scientists discovered nuclear fission - the energy released from splitting an atom - in 1938. As WWII erupted across Europe, the Allies worried that the Nazi regime might put these theoretical discoveries into action to create an atomic bomb. The United States, with support from the United Kingdom and Canada, raced to develop the weapon. President Roosevelt authorized the top-secret project in October 1941.

The researchers developed materials for two types of nuclear devices, sending them to Los Alamos, New Mexico, for conversion into a bomb. Under the supervision of scientist J. Robert Oppenheimer, the Manhattan Project held its first successful test of a nuclear bomb on July 16, 1945, in the desert near Alamogordo, New Mexico.

For President Truman, the United States had invested so much time and wealth into developing nuclear weapons that it would be difficult to justify to war-weary Americans why such a device - no matter how devastating - should not be used. The release of the nuclear bomb onto Imperial Japan would also send a warning to the Soviet Union as Stalin adopted an aggressive stance in Europe.

All this considered, President Truman gave the green light to drop the nuclear bomb on Japan to end WWII as quickly as possible.

The mission was tasked to the crew of the *Enola Gay*, a B-29 Superfortress, under the command of pilot Colonel Paul Tibbets. It lifted off on a clear day on August 6, 1945, headed to Hiroshima, Japan. The plane faced little opposition from Imperial Japan's air defenses given the strange sight of a single bomber accompanied by an observation plane rather than a large attack wave.

When the *Enola Gay* released its atomic bomb, the plane was immediately 9,000 pounds lighter. The nose of the plane leaped upward. Tibbets then put the plane into a dive to gather enough speed to put as much distance between the bomber and the spot where "Little Boy," the nickname given to the nuke, would detonate. Tibbets had 43 seconds between the release and the detonation. He pushed the *Enola Gay* as hard as he dared.

When the nuclear device exploded, Tibbets knew instantly.

The flash lit up the sky and even the interior of the plane. But it was not the blinding light that surprised Tibbets: "There was a startling sensation other than visual, however, that I remember quite vividly to this day." He recalled, "At the moment of the blast, there was a tingling sensation in my mouth and the very definite taste of lead upon my tongue. This, I was told later by scientists, was the result of electrolysis - an interaction between the fillings in my teeth and the radioactive forces that were loosed by the bomb."

The shockwave hit the *Enola Gay* as it flew nine miles from ground zero, the detonation spot. Another crew member later told reporters that "it felt as if some giant had struck the plane with a telephone pole."

As the shockwave passed, the *Enola Gay* crew knew they would safely return to base. They glanced back at Hiroshima. Tibbets and his men saw a cloud shaped like a "giant purple mushroom" reaching 45,000 feet high above the city. What they saw on the ground proved more frightening: "At the base of the cloud, fires were springing up everywhere amid a turbulent mass of smoke that had the appearance of bubbling hot tar." The transformation of the city horrified the veterans. Tibbets described the scene: "The city we had seen so clearly in the sunlight a few minutes before was now an ugly smudge. It had completely disappeared under this awful blanket of smoke and fire."

The single bomb immediately killed 80,000 people in Hiroshima. Thousands more died from radiation burns and poisoning in the coming months.

Still, Imperial Japanese leaders refused to surrender despite warnings from the United States that another bomb would be dropped.

On August 9, 1945, a second B-29 Superfortress named *Bockscar* dropped a nuclear bomb called "Fat Man" on Nagasaki, Japan. The blast immediately killed 40,000 people. Again, thousands more died over time from radiation exposure.

Japan's leaders scrambled to negotiate peace with the Allies, who bluffed that they had another nuclear weapon ready to go.

On August 15, 1945, Emperor Hirohito announced on the radio to the Japanese people that the country had surrendered.

Hearing the emperor's voice shocked the Japanese public, who considered the man divine, as it had never been broadcast before.

WWII had ended.

Did You Know . . .

- James "Cactus Jack" Garner of Texas served as Vice-President from 1933 until 1941. Prior to accepting the position under Roosevelt, he had served in the House of Representatives for 30 years. He later famously told Vice-President Lyndon Johnson: "I'll tell you, Lyndon, the vice presidency isn't worth a pitcher of warm spit."

- In preparation for the invasion of mainland Japan, the United States manufactured nearly 500,000 Purple Heart medals awarded to soldiers killed or wounded in combat.

- US Army Corps of Engineers construction projects normally received the name of the district in which the project was built. To increase secrecy, the Corps agreed to adopt the Manhattan District, referencing New York City, for its work on the atomic bomb research sites in order to confuse spies. This led to the name Manhattan Project.

- Iva Toguri, a Japanese American actress from Los Angeles, California, visited Japan in 1941, becoming stranded after the Pearl Harbor attack. Japanese officials forced Toguri to renounce her US citizenship. She soon hosted a radio program called "Zero Hour," a propaganda broadcast aimed at US soldiers who nicknamed her "Tokyo Rose." The US later convicted Toguri of treason, sentencing her to a six-year sentence.

- The formal surrender of Japan occurred on September 2, 1945, when the Japanese foreign minister boarded the battleship *USS Missouri* anchored in Tokyo's harbor. The surrender document called for Japan's unconditional surrender with US Gen. Douglas MacArthur and US Adm. Chester Nimitz overseeing the ceremony.

- The Allies occupied Japan from 1945 until 1952. However, the occupation was largely conducted by the United States under the leadership of Gen. Douglas MacArthur.

A COLD WAR

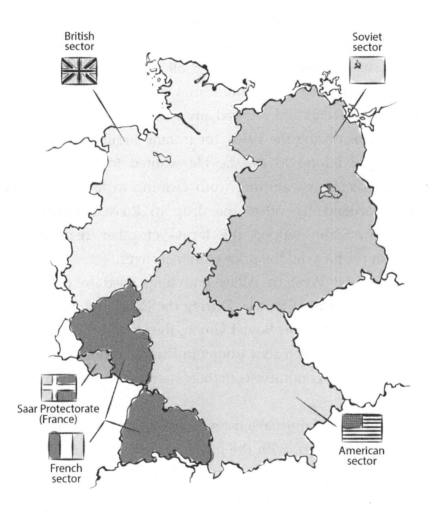

British
sector

Soviet
sector

Saar Protectorate
(France)

French
sector

American
sector

As the end of the war approached in 1945, the Allies looked to
the future. Tensions increasingly rose between the Western

Allies - led by the United States, United Kingdom, and France - and the Soviet Union.

The Western Allies had long held suspicions about the Soviet Union. As a communist country, the Soviet Union promoted an ideology that called for turning all the world to the political economy of communism. A strong centralized government would control and redistribute wealth. Though on paper communism supported equality of all and the elimination of poverty, the reality of communism was brutal as the Soviets executed opponents and silenced any criticism.

In Ukraine during the 1930s, for instance, millions starved as Stalin shipped food to Russia. He wanted to boost Russian industrial sectors by shifting from farming to factories in the Soviet heartland. To offset the drop in Russian agricultural production, Stalin tapped the farms of other regions. The Ukrainian people paid the price with their lives.

In turn, the Western Allies had long tried to overthrow communist control of Russia. During the Russian Revolution of 1917, which birthed the Soviet Union, the United States and the United Kingdom even sent troops to Russia in hopes of aiding opponents of the communists in their attempt to prevent a Soviet takeover.

These long-held mutual tensions now re-emerged in 1945.

The United States, with the nuclear bomb, had technological superiority over the Soviet Union. It also had a homeland untouched by combat. Industry and innovation flourished. This prosperity and know-how worried Stalin, who feared US efforts to undermine his communist regime.

The Soviet Union possessed the largest army in the world by the end of WWII, all with extensive combat experience. Also, the

Soviet Union had been heavily damaged by combat across its major cities, gutting much of its industrial base. This concerned Truman and his American commanders who thought the Soviets would need to seize the resources of neighboring countries to rebuild.

These shared suspicions shaped the future of Germany. Stalin feared any attempt to rebuild Germany. He wanted a Germany of rubble and Soviet control over Eastern Europe to protect the Soviet Union. Truman feared that a weak Germany would invite social upheaval and a possible communist takeover. He wanted to rebuild the war-torn country quickly as a strong buffer to absorb a possible Soviet attack on Western Europe. A rebuilt Germany on a capitalist model would also entice eastern European countries under Soviet control to resist Stalin.

To push forward Americans' plans for the global future after WWII, politicians and other officials organized the Bretton Woods Conference in July 1944. Held in Bretton Woods, New Hampshire, the US brought together Allied nations to create financial structures designed to avoid the kinds of major global depressions that had helped give rise to the Axis, especially Nazism. Obviously, the Soviet Union opposed these efforts as capitalist ploys.

Countries gathered at Bretton Woods created the World Bank and the International Monetary Fund. The World Bank provided low-interest loans to underdeveloped countries to improve their infrastructure. Such projects fostered trade and linked the countries in mutually beneficial relationships that, many believed, would reduce the risk of war. The International Monetary Fund provided emergency assistance to countries on the verge of financial collapse. This supported financial stability, heading-off potential civil wars or dictatorships.

The Allies also created the United Nations in June 1945. The organization, headquartered eventually in New York City, provided a forum for political discussion with every country in the world represented by diplomats. A Security Council formed of the major Allied powers in 1945 -the United States, United Kingdom, France, China, and the Soviet Union along with a rotation of 10 other countries elected for two-year terms - met in a permanent session to respond quickly to global crises.

Despite these achievements, the United States continued to eye the Soviet Union with suspicion. Refusals to hold open and fair elections in eastern European countries within the Soviet sphere of influence - elections agreed to by Stalin at the Yalta Conference -were evidence to Americans of the communist desire to expand across the globe.

In response, the US government adopted a policy of containment, blocking the expansion of the Soviet Union and communist regimes under Soviet influence. The concept was most vocally promoted by diplomat George Kennan, who outlined the strategy in February 1946 before elaborating on his idea in an article for the magazine *Foreign Affairs* in July 1947.

The Containment Policy was grounded on the idea that communism was a stagnant economic policy that eliminated individual initiative and creativity. To survive, communist regimes needed to seize the resources of other countries to avoid collapse.

The containment of communist countries, in Kennan's view, would quicken the failure of the Soviet Union and its puppet regimes. US officials adopted Kennan's concepts, justifying a world divided between the two superpowers with the capitalist United States on one side and the communist Soviet Union on the other side.

Acting on the containment strategy, President Truman laid out the Truman Doctrine in March 1947. The policy pledged US financial assistance to countries threatened with communist uprisings, which American officials viewed as supported by the Soviet Union.

By July 1948, Truman began funneling money to Greece and Turkey in their efforts to fight communist insurgents.

The United States also took special measures to counter the Soviet Union in Europe. President Truman and the US Congress authorized the Marshall Plan in April 1948. Named for Secretary of State George Marshall, the program provided US funds totaling $13.3 billion to rebuild war-torn Europe.

Money had to be spent on the purchase of services and materials from the US. This ensured Americans' employment in industries and Europeans' employment in construction as both returned to peacetime production. Further, a prosperous Europe would reduce the risk of war while tightening trade ties with the United States.

US dollars flowed to 18 European countries. The largest beneficiary was the United Kingdom, receiving around 26% of the funds, followed by France at 18% and West Germany at 11%.

The Plan also tried to lure Eastern Europeans to embrace a pro-American capitalist model of the future. But the Soviets refused to allow eastern European nations under its influence to accept the funds.

| Warsaw Pact | Non-aligned Nations | NATO |

Looking to keep its technological advantage over the Soviets as well as ease the transition to a peacetime economy, the US government also enacted the Servicemen's Readjustment Act in 1944. With the war over, the Act's goals were now being realized.

The Act became popularly known as the G.I. Bill. The law granted funding to veterans to attend universities and training programs. Increased knowledge of the modern world would help in the growing global tensions with the Soviet Union.

With soldiers becoming university students, the US government also avoided a sudden major spike in unemployment.

Equally important, the G. I. Bill provided low-interest loans for returning soldiers to buy new homes. With millions of men returning from overseas, a wave of new marriages occurred. Many women left wartime employment to become housewives.

A baby boom erupted during the late 1940s and early 1950s as these Americans who survived the Great Depression and WWII pursued a peaceful life of prosperity.

The American emphasis on restoring global prosperity on the capitalist model worried the Soviet leadership. In Berlin, as the western part of the city was rebuilt, Stalin expressed concerns over this part of the city becoming a beacon of change within Eastern Europe.

Stalin ordered a blockade of the roads and railroads through the Soviet-controlled eastern part of Germany to hinder any more rebuilding.

The Western Allies, led by the United States, responded with the Berlin Airlift, lasting from June 1948 until May 1949. American commanders doubted that the Soviets would risk war by shooting down planes delivering supplies to the people of Berlin.

At the peak of the operation, a plane ferrying goods landed every 45 seconds.

The Airlift carried over 2.3 million tons of supplies into the city, rendering the Soviet blockade ineffective while highlighting the might of Western air power. Soviet officials after a year restored road and railroad service rather than continue exposing the Soviet Union's weakness.

The tensions over Berlin and the reconstruction of Europe hardened the divide between the United States and the Soviet

Union. In April 1949, the North Atlantic Treaty Organization was created with an initial membership of 12 nations.

The UK, the US, and France also agreed to create a new country called West Germany in May 1949. The country was formed from their three zones of occupation, with a capital at Bonn.

The Soviet Union responded by creating East Germany out of its zone of occupation in October 1949.

The hot war against the Axis was certainly over, but an intensifying cold war between the United States and the Soviet Union threatened future conflicts.

Did You Know . . .

- The United Nations was not a new idea. US President Woodrow Wilson called for the creation of a League of Nations at the end of WWI. That organization was formed as a very weak agency that lacked the power to intervene in international disputes. The United States never joined the League because of political opposition to Wilson's idea.

- To protect its technological superiority over the Soviet Union, the United States launched Operation Paperclip after V-E Day. The operation raced to smuggle German scientists out of Soviet-controlled eastern Germany.

- To counter the North Atlantic Treaty Organization, the Soviet Union created the Warsaw Pact in May 1955. The alliance united the seven Soviet-controlled eastern European countries with the Soviet Union in a mutual defense agreement. The Pact dissolved with the collapse of the Soviet Union in 1991.

- To stop East Germans from fleeing into prosperous West Germany, the Soviet Union in August 1961 authorized the construction of the Berlin Wall, a concrete barrier around West Berlin and heavy fencing along the border with West Germany. Some 3.5 million East Germans defected from Soviet-controlled areas before the Wall, embarrassing the communist regimes of Eastern Europe.

- The United States and the Soviet Union did not directly wage war against each other during the Cold War, but they did fight proxy wars. The Soviets aided communist insurgents in Vietnam, which drew US troops into the conflict during the 1960s. On the other hand, the Americans supplied resistance fighters in Afghanistan after a Soviet invasion in 1979.

- West Germany and East Germany were reunited into a single Germany on October 3, 1990, after the collapse of the communist regime in East Germany and the fall of the Berlin Wall in 1989.

CONCLUSION

WWII had set the world ablaze. Millions of soldiers and civilians died. Beautiful and historic cities lay in ruins. Every continent except Antarctica and South America had endured at least some fighting.

The war created a new world. Old imperial powers like Britain, Holland, and France, along with aspiring imperial powers like Japan and Germany, gave way to a world dominated after 1945 by the Soviet Union and the United States. The Cold War between the two superpowers would define world affairs until the collapse of the Soviet Union in 1991.

The racist arguments grounding Nazism and Imperial Japan's expansionism pushed the Allied nations, to some extent, to confront their own racism. The Double Victory campaign in the United States sparked the civil rights movement and the end of legally recognized racial segregation by the 1960s. Colonies of the United Kingdom, France, and smaller European powers soon gained their independence, including India, Pakistan, and Indonesia, among many others. The United States finally granted independence to the Philippines; a country overseen by the Americans from 1898 until 1946.

The Holocaust particularly served as a reminder of the destructive outcomes of racist ideologies. Former death camps like Auschwitz became memorial sites preserved to teach future generations about the need for peace and equality. The

Nuremberg Trials developed international law on human rights and war crimes.

Our world today continues to live under the shadow of WWII. The United Nations actively sends peacekeepers into conflict zones to limit outbreaks of war and genocide, as in Bosnia and Rwanda in the 1990s. The North Atlantic Treaty Organization, now with over 30 member countries, maintains peace in Europe and has acted against aggressive actions like those of Russia after it invaded non-member Ukraine in 2022.

The United Nations also provides a forum for discussion of measures to counter climate change and other global concerns. The World Bank has aided struggling countries to improve their infrastructure, from roads to healthcare systems. The International Monetary Fund has supplied emergency funding to rescue countries from economic collapse, as in Greece in 2010. Oversight of such loans and other financial assistance has required aided countries to act more vigorously against corruption or inefficient practices.

The sacrifices of those who fought and won WWII laid the foundation for a better world. It is for this reason that Americans refer to them as the Greatest Generation.

Made in the USA
Las Vegas, NV
10 December 2024

13831599R00095